Edward Lear and the Art of Travel

Edward Lear and the Art of Travel

Scott Wilcox

WITH CONTRIBUTIONS BY

Eva Bowerman
Clay Dean
Morna O'Neill
Stephen Vella
Emily Weeks

Yale Center for British Art

Published on the occasion of an exhibition
Yale Center for British Art, New Haven, Connecticut,
September 20, 2000–January 14, 2001

© 2000 Yale Center for British Art
ISBN 0-930606-92-2
Library of Congress Contol Number: 00-132667

Design and Composition by group c INC
Printed by Herlin Press Inc.
Photography by Richard Caspole, with the exception of
cat. 59, 162, 173 and 174, which are reproduced with permission
of the Beinecke Rare Book and Manuscript Library, Yale University

Map on pages 43, 53, 68, 81 and 117: *Map of the Overland Routes
between England and India*, London, W.H. Allen, 1842.

Cat. 100   *Amada*, 6:50 am, 12 February 1867 (419)   inside back cover
Cat. 101   *Amada*, 7:10 am, 12 February 1867 (420)   back cover
Cat. 102   *Amada*, 7:20 am, 12 February 1867 (421)   front cover
Cat. 103   *Amada*, 7:25 am, 12 February 1867 (422)   inside front cover
Cat. 104   *Amada*, 7:30 am, 12 February 1867 (423)   half title page

Contents

Foreword   6
PATRICK McCAUGHEY

Acknowledgments   7

Introduction   9
SCOTT WILCOX

"To Topographize all the Journeyings of my Life"   13
SCOTT WILCOX

Catalogue
PART ONE: Edward Lear   43
PART TWO: British Artists Abroad   117

Selected Bibliography   189

Foreword

Donald Gallup enjoys an international reputation as the foremost bibliographer of T. S. Eliot and Ezra Pound. He enjoys a wide national reputation as the distinguished Elizabeth Wakeman Dwight Curator Emeritus of the Collection of American Literature at the Beinecke Rare Book and Manuscript Library. At the Yale Center for British Art, he enjoys the reputation of the largest single donor to the collection apart from our founder, Paul Mellon, for his gift in 1997 and 1998 of nine oil paintings, over 350 drawings and prints, manuscripts and memorabilia of Edward Lear. The magnitude and generosity of Donald Gallup's gift gave Paul Mellon special pleasure. When Donald Gallup gave his Lear collection, the Yale Center for British Art decided to mount an exhibition, setting Lear into the wider context of the art of travel. *Edward Lear and the Art of Travel* is the happy result, with virtually the entire exhibition drawn from the permanent collection of the Center. It both illustrates the depth of its resources and demonstrates how a munificent gift like Donald Gallup's can provide a new direction and a new focus for the collection as a whole.

Travel, the record and experience of travelers, has long been a staple interest of British art history from the Grand Tourists of the eighteenth century to the romantic questers of the early nineteenth century. Victorian travel and travelers have rapidly caught up with these early and familiar themes. Travel in the glow of Empire and the light of science, the first glimmerings of the encounter with "the other" and the awareness of the antiquity of non-Western civilizations, all form a rich seam of images in nineteenth-century British art and literature.

The Center is profoundly grateful to Donald Gallup for his gift and for providing the impetus for this exhibition. It makes a start in the examination and the analysis of some new, challenging and exciting themes. Where Edward Lear may once unfairly have been regarded as a curious, delightful but marginal British artist, it is our happy experience to place him at the very center of one of the most important threads in Victorian art and experience.

Patrick McCaughey
Director

Acknowledgments

Exhibitions are communal enterprises, dependent for their success on the efforts of a host of people. I would like to express my gratitude to all my colleagues at the Yale Center for British Art who have brought to the project their customary intelligence, creativity, and unstinting hard work. Special thanks are due to my fellow authors of the catalogue, all graduate students at Yale University, and to Shira Brisman, a Yale undergraduate, who, as Duncan Robinson Fellow in the summer of 1999, provided invaluable organizational and research assistance. Anne Anninger, formerly Philip Hofer Curator of Printing and Graphic Arts at the Houghton Library of Harvard University, and other members of the Houghton staff graciously met my research needs there. Vincent Giroud, Curator of Modern Books and Manuscripts, and the staff of the Beinecke Rare Book and Manuscript Library were extremely helpful in providing loans which allowed us to represent the role of photography in mid-nineteenth-century travel art. Finally, I would like to extend a personal note of thanks to Donald Gallup, who, in addition to his generosity as a donor, proffered much useful information and cast a knowledgeable eye over the catalogue text. SW

54

54 Edward Lear (1812-1888)

Zagóri, Greece, 1860

Oil on canvas

Introduction

On a winter afternoon in wartime London, the attention of a young American officer walking down Museum Street near the British Museum was attracted by several small watercolors displayed in a shop window. The officer was Donald C. Gallup, a graduate of Yale and an English teacher, at the time serving in the Adjutant General's section of the United States Army Services of Supply Headquarters. The shop was that of the printseller, F. R. Meatyard. The watercolors were sketches by Edward Lear.[1]

Two tremendous caches of drawings by Lear had come on the market within months of one another in 1929. The first had been bequeathed by Lear to his friend and executor, Franklin Lushington; the second given by Lear to Lord Northbrook. Many of these drawings were acquired by the American collectors Philip Hofer and W. B. Osgood Field and given by them to the Houghton Library at Harvard in 1942. Craddock & Barnard in Tunbridge Wells obtained a sizeable group of the drawings, and the selection of Lear drawings that captivated Gallup came to Meatyard's from them.

As a student of English literature, Gallup had known of Lear's nonsense verses, and Angus Davidson's 1939 biography had acquainted him with Lear's career as an artist. After purchasing one or two small drawings (priced at only a few shillings each) on that winter afternoon, Gallup returned to the shop regularly, buying a few more drawings each week. The visits to Meatyard's culminated in the purchase of an album of 340 watercolor sketches of 1867, mostly from Lear's trip up the Nile early in that year (cat. 60-123). From London bookshops, Gallup also acquired Lear's published topographical volumes. Before he returned to the United States in the closing days of 1945, he bought another album, this one containing thirty-four early landscape drawings by Lear.

In 1947 Gallup became the Curator of the Yale Collection of American Literature, a position that he would occupy with distinction for thirty-three years. During those years he was instrumental in bringing many important archives and collections of literary papers to Yale. In his personal collecting, he continued from time to time to add to the Lear material he had acquired during the war. An oil sketch (cat. 16) had been included in the album of drawings he purchased in December 1945. He acquired his first finished oil painting, *Zagóri, Greece* (cat. 54), in London in 1949, and his largest, the grand *Kangchenjunga from Darjeeling* (cat. 130), which had belonged to W. B. Osgood Field, in New York in 1951. To the books, he was able to add copies of *Gleanings from the Menagerie and Aviary at Knowsley Hall,* 1846, and *Tortoises, Terrapins & Turtles,* 1872. In the area of Lear's nonsense illustration, Gallup purchased eight drawings, unpublished at the time, illustrating "St. Kiven and the Gentle Kathleen" by the Irish poet Thomas Moore (cat. 49).

In early 1997 Donald Gallup gave his Lear collection to the Yale Center for British Art. Consisting of nine oil paintings, 356 watercolors and drawings, and twenty-eight prints, this was the largest and most valuable gift to the Center after the benefaction of its founder Paul Mellon. Added to the small but choice group of paintings and drawings by Lear that had already been given by Mellon and a few other donors,

1 This introduction draws on Donald Gallup's more complete and charmingly personal account of his collecting of the work of Edward Lear in the second volume of his memoirs, *What Mad Pursuits! More Memories of a Yale Librarian* (New Haven: The Beinecke Rare Book and Manuscript Library, 1998), pp. 69-89.

49 Edward Lear (1812-1888)

St. Kiven and the Gentle Kathleen

Pen and brown ink on laid paper

49

the Center now boasted one of the outstanding collections of the art of this remarkable figure to be found anywhere. Although it can by no means match the depth or the sheer scale of the holdings at the Houghton Library, the Lear collection at the Yale Center for British Art not only contains beautiful and representative examples of Lear's art but also has the advantage of being placed within the context of a uniquely comprehensive collection of British travel art and illustrated travel books.

Gallup's gift was followed almost immediately by the decision of the Center's director, Patrick McCaughey, to mount an exhibition celebrating Gallup's generosity. But what form should the exhibition take? From the 1940s on, there have been a number of exhibitions devoted to Lear, most lavishly and extensively, the exhibition at the Royal Academy of Arts in London in 1985 that was shown subsequently at the National Academy of Design in New York. That exhibition, organized by the preeminent authority on Lear, Vivien Noakes, covered all aspects of Lear's life, including juvenilia, memorabilia, and large sections devoted to the natural history drawings and the nonsense verse. For the Yale Center for British Art, it seemed to make sense to capitalize on the strength of Gallup's collection by concentrating on Lear as a topographical artist. And by capitalizing on the position of the Lear collection within the Center's larger collections, the Center could do something that no earlier Lear exhibition had done—it could place his topographical art within the vast outpouring of images of foreign lands created by British artist travelers of the later eighteenth and nineteenth centuries.

Almost every account of the art of Edward Lear begins with the comment that he is better known as the author of nonsense verse. This is usually followed by the treatment of his artistic output as the extraordinary isolated product of a remarkable Victorian eccentric. It is the intent of this catalogue and exhibition to bring Lear's art out of isolation, so that it may once again jostle for attention with the other art produced by his predecessors and contemporaries to appeal to a travel-hungry public. Far from downplaying Lear's eccentricity and the remarkableness of his art, they appear enhanced. In considering Lear's drawings and paintings against the backdrop of broader currents in topography and landscape art, I cannot claim to be charting an entirely new course. Philip Hofer in his *Edward Lear as Landscape Draughtsman,* 1967, included a chapter "The Tradition of Landscape Drawing that Lear Inherited." For the catalogue of the exhibition at the Royal Academy in 1985, Jeremy Maas provided a short essay titled "From the Sublime to the Ridiculous: Edward Lear in his Artistic Context." Most fruitful in this vein is Allen Staley's essay "The Painter of Topographical Poetry" in the catalogue for another Lear exhibition, *Impossible Picturesqueness: Edward Lear's Indian Watercolours, 1873-1875.* This exhibition attempts to flesh out their observations, and this catalogue seeks to amplify and extend their insights.

Anyone taking pen to paper to write about Edward Lear feels a tremendous debt to Vivien Noakes, that, and a humbling sense of being superfluous. Her numerous writings on Lear, including *Edward Lear: The Life of a Wanderer,* 1968, the aforementioned Royal Academy catalogue, and *The Painter Edward Lear,* 1991, provide a detailed and compelling portrait of the man and the artist. The essay that follows draws heavily on all three. It focuses specifically on Lear's experience and achievement as an artist traveler and on the environment of travel art in which he operated.

In drawing on the rich resources of the Yale Center for British Art, I have necessarily been highly selective. Using Lear's own wanderings as a rough guide, I have deliberately limited the scope to works depicting the Mediterranean and India. I have defined "artist traveler" in this instance as the professional artist, as Lear considered himself to be, mostly excluding that large body of talented amateurs—military officers, diplomats, businessmen, and tourists—who documented their travels in works of considerable charm and even greater historical interest. Even within these limits I have taken an impressionistic approach. For example, the extensive and richly textured presentation of illustrated travel literature that the rare books collection at the Center would make possible is only suggested by the selection of volumes that space permitted.

Since the publication of Edward Said's immensely influential *Orientalism* in 1978, there has been growing scholarly interest in the ways in which western artists, writers, and thinkers have represented, defined, and thereby sought to control or contain non-western cultures. Lear and his fellow artist travelers carried with them assumptions about their place in the world and about their relationships with the indigenous peoples among whom they passed. The landscapes in this exhibition often subtly, sometimes blatantly, embody these attitudes and assumptions. While acknowledging the value and relevance of reading these landscapes as texts in the construction of an imperial worldview, I take as my own focus the internal dynamics of the topographical tradition and Lear's role within that tradition.

130 Edward Lear (1812-1888)

Kangchenjunga from Darjeeling, 1879

Oil on canvas

"To Topographize All the Journeyings of My Life"

To one friend, Edward Lear described himself as the "Topographical Artist."[1] To another, he characterized himself as "a painter of poetical topography."[2] To a third, he wrote of his goal "to topographize and topographize all the journeyings of my life, so that I shall have been of some use after all to my fellow critters besides leaving the drawings and pictures which they may sell when I'm dead."[3] These three statements, to which others by Lear could be added, testify to the centrality of the topographical enterprise to Lear's conception of himself as an artist. At the same time, they signal the complications inherent in both Lear's self-conception and in the idea of topography itself.

The place that Edward Lear occupies in the long tradition of topographical painting, draftsmanship, and printmaking is an important but uneasy one. For his friend Charles Church, Lear's "description of himself as the 'Topographical Artist' marked his purpose of making truth and fidelity the special object in his work, without attempting to give to his landscape effects of his own device or imagination which did not belong to the scenery of that particular region, or, as he said, to make 'fiction for the delight of those who prefer prettiness to truth.'"[4] Poetry and truth need not be incompatible; poetry and topography were frequently thought to be. With his claim to be a painter of poetical topography, Lear situates himself both within the utilitarian documentary tradition and above it. His ambition in painting grand landscapes, embodied most strikingly in a work such as *Kangchenjunga from Darjeeling* (cat. 130), was to infuse his informational content with an epic visual poetry, without the poetry obscuring or falsifying the information. His models were the paintings of Joseph Mallord William Turner and later the American Frederic Edwin Church.

Lear's comment on topographizing the journeyings of his life as something separate from his drawing and pictures indicates that, for all his ambition to be recognized as a landscape painter in oils, he felt the limitations of the visual image in the informational project that he had set for himself. Charles Church again corroborates, writing of Lear's desire to publish the journals of his travels to accompany his illustrations as "the best method, when read in combination with the illustration annexed, of giving a clear idea of the scenes."[5] As Church noted, "the combination of journal and drawing form part of his plans as 'Topographical Artist.'"[6] Lear's concern with providing a textual framework for his picture-making and with creating a topographical art from the alliance of word and image can be understood as reflecting his need to find a niche for his work within the ever growing library of travel literature, much of it lavishly illustrated, available to the British public in the nineteenth century. Indeed, Lear's artistic achievements can be most fully appreciated and the tensions, contradictions and complexities of his practice as an artist best understood within the changing context of work by British artist travelers from the middle of the eighteenth century to the end of the nineteenth. At the same time Lear's efforts to create a meaningful art and to make a living from it provide a lens through which we can valuably survey the broader topographical tradition.

1 Quoted in Vivien Noakes, *The Painter Edward Lear* (London: David and Charles, 1991), p. 9.

2 Letter to Chichester Fortescue, August 22, 1881, *Later Letters of Edward Lear*, edited by Lady Constance Strachey (London: T. Fisher Unwin, 1911), p. 245.

3 Letter to Lady Waldegrave, January 9, 1868, Ibid., p. 91.

4 Quoted in Noakes 1991, p. 9.

5 Lear quoted by Church, in Noakes 1991, pp. 15-16.

6 Quoted in Noakes 1991, p. 16.

7   In addition to Vivien Noakes, *Edward Lear: The Life of a Wanderer* (London: Collins, 1968), other biographies include Angus Davidson, *Edward Lear, Landscape Painter and Nonsense Poet* (New York: Dutton, 1939), John Lehman, *Edward Lear and His World* (London: Thames and Hudson, 1977), Susan Chitty, *That Singular Person Called Lear* (London: Weidenfield and Nicolson, 1988), and Peter Levi, *Edward Lear: A Biography* (London: Macmillan, 1995).

Lear was born in Holloway near London in 1812.[7] The twentieth of twenty-one children, he was raised and taught by his eldest sister Ann. He had no formal education. Having taught himself to draw, he published in parts between 1830 and 1832 his *Illustrations of the Family of Psittacidae, or Parrots* (see cat. 1), which established his reputation as an ornithological draftsman. As a result of his works on parrots, he was invited by Lord Stanley, later the thirteenth Earl of Derby, to draw the birds and animals in the menagerie at Knowsley Hall, near Liverpool. His association with Derby and the aristocratic circles to which he was introduced had important and long-lasting consequences for Lear.

Although Lear continued to work as a natural history draftsman until 1837, he had begun to change direction several years earlier. Through working on his lithographs of parrots in the studio of the lithographer Charles Hullmandel, he had met the landscape painters J. M. W. Turner, Clarkson Stanfield, and James Duffield Harding. By 1834 he was drawing landscapes of his own, quickly developing a style, which, though highly reliant on the popular manner of Harding, was effective and sensitive. The scientific bent and habits of detailed observation Lear had acquired in his natural history work carried over into his approach to landscape; however, the close correspondence of observed fact to drawn mark that characterizes natural history draftsmanship — the degree of detailed observation and precise draftsmanship required for the accurate rendering of plumage which placed such a strain on Lear's weak eyes — is an impossibility in the representing of landscape. The landscape artist must perforce rely on conventions and schemata. What is impressive about the series of graphite and white gouache drawings on gray paper that Lear brought back from a tour of the Lake District in 1836 (cat. 8-13) is, on the one hand, how completely he has made the conventions derived from Harding his own, and, on the other, how his individual vision, perhaps more scientific than picturesque, keeps his images from seeming stale or simply imitative.

Lear enrolled at Sass's School of Art in Charlotte Street, Bloomsbury, where, like his fellow students, William Frith and Augustus Egg, he prepared himself to enter the Royal Academy Schools. He did not in fact become a student at the Royal Academy until 1850. Instead, in 1837 the Earl of Derby and his nephew Robert Hornby undertook to send Lear to Rome. Apart from return visits to Britain in the summer and autumn of 1841 and again in the summer of 1845, Lear remained in Italy for over a decade. During his first years in Italy, he continued to employ and refine the conventional Harding-like style of draftsmanship both in finished drawings in soft graphite or black chalk with white gouache on colored paper and in lithographs published as *Views in Rome and its Environs* (cat. 22-25) in 1841 and *Illustrated Excursions in Italy* (cat. 32) in 1846. In his last years in Italy he developed the distinctive sketching style that has come to characterize his art. A pencil outline drawing complete with annotations as to color and features of the landscape done on the spot, would later have watercolor washes added and both the outlines and the annotations gone over in pen and ink, a process he referred to as "penning-out." These elaborated sketches were not considered by Lear to be finished, saleable works of art. They did, however, have a public role; Lear exhibited them to potential patrons to encourage the commissioning of finished

13

23

13   Edward Lear (1812-1888)

Ullswater, 14 Oct. 1836

Graphite with stump and white gouache
on gray wove paper

23   Edward Lear (1812-1888)

Valmontone, from *Views in Rome and
its Environs,* 1841

Lithograph

16 Edward Lear (1812-1888)

Corpo di Cava, 28 June 1838

Oil on gray wove paper

16

watercolors or oil paintings. Lear made his first attempts at oil painting in 1838, sketches of vegetation at Corpo di Cava (cat. 16). By the time he left Italy in 1848, oil painting had replaced drawing as the focus of his artistic aspirations.

Responding to the unsettled political situation in Italy and his own combination of restlessness and a desire to be settled, Lear was by the beginning of 1848 anxious to extend his travels into the eastern Mediterranean but also to return to England. He visited Corfu in response to an invitation from George Bowen, President of the University of Corfu. From there, as a result of a series of additional invitations from friends and acquaintances, Lear traveled to Athens, to Constantinople, across northern Greece and Albania, to Egypt, and back to Greece — a quite extaordinary odyssey — before returning to England in the summer of 1849.

33

33 Edward Lear (1812-1888)

View near Palermo, 1847

Pen and brown ink with watercolor
over graphite

Intent on establishing himself as a landscape painter but painfully conscious of the deficiencies of his artistic training, Lear sought entry into the Royal Academy Schools and was admitted in 1850, although he seems not to have remained a student there for long. Before leaving Italy, when he was still undecided as to his immediate plans, he had written to his friend Chichester Fortescue: "I am in a disturbidous state along of my being undecided as to how I shall go on with art—knowing that figure drawing is that which I know least of & yet is the 'crown & roof of things'.—Sometimes I plan working hard all this spring & summer at figure drawing."[8] Instead he traveled east, but six months later, on the banks of the Bosphorus, he wrote again: "What to do, my Dear Fortescue when I return to England!!??¿ - ¿! (expressive of indelible doubt, wonder, & ignorance.) London must be the place, & then comes the choice of two lines; society, & half days work, pretty pictures, petitmâitre praise boundless, frequented studio &c., &c. wound up with vexation of spirit as age comes on that talents have been thrown away:—or *hard*

8 Letter to Fortescue, February 12, 1848, Edward Lear,
Selected Letters, edited by Vivien Noakes (Oxford:
Clarendon Press, 1988) pp. 67-8.

37 Edward Lear (1812-1888)

Near Suez, 1 pm, 16 January 1849 (48)

Pen and brown ink with watercolor
over graphite

37

9 Letter to Fortescue, August 25, 1848, *Letters of Edward Lear,* edited by Lady Constance Strachey (London: T. Fisher Unwin, 1907), pp.13-14.

10 Quoted in Noakes 1991, p. 59.

11 William Holman Hunt, *Pre-Raphaelitism and the Pre-Raphaelite Brotherhood* (London: MacMillan, 1905), vol. 1, p. 328.

study beginning at the root of the matter, the human figure, which to master alone would enable me to carry out the views & feelings of landscape I know to exist within me. Alas! if real art is a *student,* I know no more than a child, an infant, a foetus. How could I. I have had myself to thank for all education, & a vortex of society hath eaten my time."[9] Lear chose the route of hard study, and even if the process was painful and shortlived, he did acknowledge its usefulness. In a diary entry a decade later he wrote: "Rejoiced at my slavy labours at anatomy in 1849-50 — for small progress as I made — I can make somewhat like figures now — & never could before."[10]

In 1852 he met the Pre-Raphaelite painter William Holman Hunt. Lear looked to the younger Hunt for guidance in painting, and Hunt's strictures on working directly from nature must have resonated with both Lear's natural history background and his feelings of inadequacy as a painter. Looking over the pen and ink and watercolor sketches which Lear hoped to use as the basis for oil paintings, Hunt commented: "I could not and would not attempt to paint pictures in a studio from such mere skeleton outlines."[11] At Hunt's suggestion, Lear carted his large canvas of the *Quarries of Syracuse* from one spot in the south of England to another in order to paint "from nature" the rocks and vegetation of this Sicilian view— a rather elastic conception of truth to nature. For a few weeks that summer, the two artists worked

56

56 Edward Lear (1812-1888)
Corfu from Santa Decca, 1862
Oil on canvas

together near Hastings, painting directly from nature, a practice Lear doggedly followed that summer and the next. Lear subsequently abandoned the practice, producing his paintings in the studio on the basis of sketches as he had intended before Hunt's intervention. But he continued to look up to Hunt, and the two remained friends.

With his health and spirits both suffering from English weather and with the public and critical reaction to his oil paintings disappointing, Lear revised his plan to settle in England. Apart from periodic return visits to England, he largely lived abroad for the rest of his life. In 1853-54 he made another visit to Egypt. Towards the end of 1855 he returned to Corfu, which became something of a base of operations for him until the British return of the Ionian Islands to Greece in 1864. After attempts to establish himself in Nice, Malta, and Cannes proved unsatisfactory, he settled in San Remo on the Italian Riviera. There in 1870 he purchased land overlooking the sea and built a house with a studio and a gallery. In 1872 he was invited to visit India by his friend George Baring, Lord Northbrook, who had been appointed viceroy. After an abortive attempt that got Lear as far as Suez, he did make the journey the following year, spending fifteen months traveling through the subcontinent and Ceylon. It was his last major sketching tour. His final years were occupied with a long cherished project to illustrate the poems of his friend

137 Edward Lear (1812-1888)

Areka Palms, Ratnapoora, Ceylon, c. 1884-85

Pen and black ink and gray wash
on wove paper mounted on card

190 Samuel Prout (1783-1852)

Sketches in France, Switzerland and Italy
London: Hodgson and Graves, 1839

Shown: *The Forum, Rome*
Lithograph by Charles Hullmandel

137

190

180

180   James Duffield Harding (1798-1863)

Sketches at Home and Abroad
London: Charles Tilt, 1836

Shown: *Como from the Milan Road*
Lithograph printed by Charles Hullmandel

Alfred Lord Tennyson with landscape subjects. The construction of a hotel in San Remo blocking Lear's view of the sea caused him to sell his house, which he called Villa Emily, and to build another in 1881, which he named Villa Tennyson. It was there that he died on January 29, 1888.

℘

If we consider the publication of Lear's *Views in Rome and Its Environs* in 1841 as marking the real start of his career as a topographical artist, he was launching himself at a propitious moment. Travel art, while inheriting the traditions of eighteenth-century topography, was responding to new audiences by embracing new forms and new content. Certainly Lear would be able to find a place within this flourishing and varied field.

In 1839, Samuel Prout published his *Sketches in France, Switzerland and Italy* (cat. 190), the long-delayed sequel to his *Facsimiles of Sketches made in Flanders and Germany* of 1833. The *Facsimiles of Sketches made in Flanders and Germany* had launched the fashion for sets of lithographic views of foreign subjects, so successfully exploited by artists such as James Duffield Harding and David Roberts.[12] It was also the volume that inspired the Ruskin family's first tour abroad. Though much appreciated and admired by John Ruskin and acknowledged by Roberts as an important influence — Roberts wrote to Prout in 1833,

12   Prout's first great success in lithography was his *Illustrations of the Rhine* of 1824, but in its tonal use of the medium, it was less effective in communicating the character of pencil drawing than the later *Facsimiles of Sketches Made in Flanders and Germany.* In that regard, it was the later volume that proved more influential.

192

24

192 David Roberts (1796-1864)

Picturesque Sketches in Spain
London: Hodgson and Graves, 1837

Shown: *Tower of Comares, the Fortress of Alhambra*

Lithograph printed by Charles Hullmandel

24 Edward Lear (1812-1888)

Campagna of Rome from Villa Mattei, from *Views in Rome and its Environs*, 1841

Lithograph

"I founded what little I possess on your good works"[13]— Prout's drawing style, as reflected in the lithographs of *Sketches in France, Switzerland and Italy,* seemed old-fashioned in comparison to the publications of his younger colleagues. In 1836 Harding had brought out his *Sketches at Home and Abroad* (cat. 180), in which he pioneered with the lithographer Charles Hullmandel the use of a tint stone to capture the look of a drawing on tinted paper heightened with Chinese white.[14] J. F. Lewis, working with Hullmandel, had employed the technique of the tinted lithograph in the illustrated volumes on Spain that he published in 1836 (see cat. 183), as had Roberts, working again with Hullmandel, in his Spanish volume of thirty-seven lithographs the following year (cat. 192). Roberts enjoyed extraordinary success with his *Picturesque Sketches in Spain;* twelve hundred volumes were sold in two months. The popularity of these publications must have been much in Lear's mind, as he produced the tinted lithographs for his own *Views in Rome and Its Environs* (cat. 22-25) in Hullmandel's workshop. In 1841 Roberts was at work on his drawings for the *Holy Land,* the first volume of which would appear the following year. When completed as *The Holy Land, Syria, Idumea, Arabia, Egypt & Nubia* in 1849, this collection of 247 lithographs would stand as one of the greatest monuments of nineteenth-century travel art and art publishing.[15]

Much less lavish and prestigious than these lithographic volumes, but much more widely disseminated, were the "annuals," introduced in England in 1823 by the German émigré publisher Rudolph Ackermann. These small anthologies of prose and poetry illustrated with steel engravings were intended for year-end gift giving. While some were miscellanies of art and writing, others were specifically topographical, taking a particular country or region as theme and employing a single author and illustrator. Samuel Prout again played a key role in the development of the "annual." He contributed illustrations to a number of these volumes in the 1820s and 1830s and was the sole illustrator for the first two *Landscape Annuals*, in 1830 and 1831, both of which were devoted to Italy. For the third *Landscape Annual*, also devoted to Italy, Prout was replaced as illustrator by J. D. Harding, occasioning a bitter and longstanding rift between the two artists. The production of topographical illustrations for popular publications was lucrative and consequently highly competitive. Roberts provided illustrations of Spain for *Landscape Annuals* in 1835, 1836, and 1837, and of Spain and Morocco in 1838.[16] There were also the editions of poetry, such as Samuel Rogers' *Italy*, Murray's *The Life and Works of Byron*, and Finden's *Landscape Illustrations to the Life and Works of Lord Byron*, illustrated with steel engravings after topographical drawings by Turner and others, which provided a precedent for Lear's long-cherished project of illustrating Tennyson.

In London's annual exhibitions, topographical representations of the Continent and subjects further afield had a small but distinct presence. John "Warwick" Smith, one of the noted topographical draftsmen of the later eighteenth century, had been elected to the Old Water-Colour Society in 1806, just two years after its foundation, acknowledgement of his status as one of the grand old men of the watercolor movement. His imposing *The Colosseum, Rome* (cat. 158) was shown at the Society's exhibition the following year. From 1820 Prout's watercolors of Continental subjects were a mainstay of the Society's exhibitions, a subject specialty in which he would be joined by Harding and William Callow and a few other younger artists. In 1841 Prout contributed twenty watercolors and Callow eight — all Continental views — though Harding's three submissions that year were of British scenery. There were only a handful of topographical paintings in the Royal Academy exhibition for 1841, most of those views of Italy, including three paintings of Venice by Turner. Roberts, who had exhibited his topographical oil paintings at the Royal Academy since 1826 (and at the British Institution and the Society of British Artists before that), was elected Royal Academician in 1841. In the Academy's exhibition that year he showed two oil paintings derived from his trip to the Middle East, *Portico of the Temple of Dendera, in Upper Egypt* and *Jerusalem from the Mount of Olives*.

Another Middle Eastern view was the subject of a more broadly popular form of exhibition. From December 1840 to March 1842 *View of the City of Damascus and the Surrounding Country* was on display at the Leicester Square Panorama. The spectacle of the panorama, with its vast 360° views presented in purpose-built rotundas, had been developed in the late eighteenth-century by Robert Barker and his son

13 Quoted in Richard Lockett, *Samuel Prout, 1783-1852* (London: Batsford, 1985), p. 9

14 For the contributions of Hullmandel and Harding to the art of lithography, see Christine Swenson, *Charles Hullmandel and James Duffield Harding: A Study of the English Art of Drawing on Stone, 1818-1850*, exhibition catalogue (Northampton: Smith College Museum of Art, 1982). An article in the *Art-Union*, October 15, 1839, p. 146, titled "The Progress of Painting in Water Colours," credited Harding with the introduction of opaque white in watercolor painting.

15 *Travel in Aquatint and Lithography, 1770-1860, from the Library of J. R. Abbey* (London: Curwen Press, 1957) vol. 2, pp. 334-341 provides a full account of the work's publication history.

16 For the development of the *Landscape Annual*, see Lockett, pp. 77-80, and Michael Pidgley, "Travel, Topography, and Prints," in Helen Guiterman and Briony Llewellyn, *David Roberts*, exhibition catalogue (London: Barbican Art Gallery, 1986), pp. 47-65.

158 John "Warwick" Smith (1749-1831)

The Colosseum, Rome, 1802

Watercolor over graphite

158

Henry Aston Barker. Although topographical in nature from the outset, the panorama was originally presented by its promoters primarily as an experiment in versimilitude and a serious advance in the art of painting. By the early nineteenth century, with the rise of a host of imitators and rivals to their establishment in Leicester Square, the Barkers repositioned their scenic entertainment as a serious source of information about the outside world. Successfully capitalizing on the public's taste for foreign views, particularly at a time when opportunities for travel abroad were severely curtailed by the Napoleonic wars, they moved beyond their initial presentations of British cities and recent naval victories to offer views of foreign locales, the first of which was Constantinople, shown in 1801-1802 (see cat. 161). The Barkers and their successors purveyed a mix of illusionism, exoticism, and educational uplift in a series of panoramas that eventually ranged in subject from Macao in China to the Polar Regions and continued to attract audiences to the rotunda in Leicester Square until 1863.[17]

From the gargantuan spectacle of the panoramas to the intimate experience of the steel-engraved illustrations in the landscape annuals, the consumption of travel art in the 1820s, '30s, and '40s, was fueled by the expansion of the audience for art (both public and domestic) and the expansion of tourism (both

17 The Leicester Square Panorama as a vehicle for bringing foreign locales before a British audience is treated in Scott Wilcox, "The Panorama of Leicester Square" in *European Traveler-Artists in Nineteenth-Century Mexico,* exhibition catalogue (Mexico City: Fomento Cultural Banamex, 1996), pp. 127-135. For other volumes on the panorama, see the note to cat. 161.

the actual and the arm-chair varieties). When British travel on the Continent and around the Mediterranean resumed after the lengthy enforced hiatus of the wars with France, it was a different phenomenon from the Grand Tour of the eighteenth century. Although it seemed at times to eighteenth-century Italians, and to visiting Britons, that Italy was overrun by British tourists, the Grand Tour was an exclusive undertaking, available only to a small cultured elite. Through the first half of the nineteenth century, the experience of traveling abroad became available to a widening segment of the British public, and the actual number of travelers began that steady ascent towards the throngs in the second half of the century, the age of the Cook's Tour, and to the mass tourism of the century just passed. The numbers were greater, but nineteenth-century tourism in Italy followed in many respects the patterns of the Grand Tour. And though Iberia and Greece loomed large in the Romantic imagination, and the archaeological discoveries and biblical associations of the Holy Land and Egypt claimed the attention of the devout, Italy remained the most popular destination in the Mediterranean for British tourists.[18] Of course, artists were called upon to supply not just souvenirs of places visited but images of places that were tantalizingly out of reach to most of their audience. In a crowded field, novelty was a positive virtue. While Lear's *Views in Rome and Its Environs* contains many views that would have been familiar to most British tourists to Italy, in his second publication, *Illustrated Excursions in Italy,* he is already concentrating on the little known view and seldom visited site.

18 See John Pemble, *The Mediterranean Passion: Victorians and Edwardians in the South* (Oxford: Clarendon Press, 1987), for patterns of nineteenth-century British tourism in the Mediterranean.

ᴄʌ

The popular travel art of the 1840s is almost unrecognizable as the descendant of the art of eighteenth-century topographers, patronized by touring milords and learned antiquaries. Yet the art of Prout, Harding, Roberts, and Lear arose from foundations laid in the eighteenth century by topographical draftsmen, on the one hand, and painters of ideal landscape, on the other. For Lear, as for many of his contemporaries, the greatest exponent of landscape painting was J. M. W. Turner, who had inherited and transformed the lineage of ideal landscape painting, stretching back to the seventeenth-century masters, Claude, Poussin, and Rosa. Turner's beginnings lay in topographical draftsmanship, and part, though only part, of the transformation that he had effected in landscape consisted of fusing the formulations and lofty ideals of classical landscape with the concrete specificity of topography. In the eighteenth-century the distinction between ideal and topographic landscape painting, though hardly an impermeable boundary, was marked. Ideal landscape was evocative and allusive, redolent of the classical world, frequently the setting for events of mythology and history. Topography was scientific and antiquarian; it was the offspring not of old master picture-making but of cartography; its values were clarity, accuracy and completeness. Although the topographer might be a painter, he was more likely to be a draftsman or an illustrator, his work less likely to be found hanging framed on the wall than in an antiquarian's portfolio. The characteristic form of the "stained" or "tinted" drawing, in which pen and ink outlines defined the features of a monument or view while subtle washes of watercolor conveyed mass and light, was ideally and elegantly suited to the informational needs of topography.

149 Williams Pars (1742-1782)

Temple of Venus and Rome, Rome, 1781

Watercolor with pen and brown ink
over graphite on laid paper

149

Most imaginative landscape painting was based on an idealized version of the Italian landscape, frequently incorporating actual features of that landscape and the architectural remains of Roman antiquity. Richard Wilson, who did more than anyone else to establish landscape painting as a serious form of high art in late Georgian Britain, amassed a store of motifs during his years of study in Rome in the 1750s that he would deploy in his grand landscape visions painted back in London. On the other hand, topographical draftsmen such as William Pars, whose stay in Rome from 1775 to his death in 1782 was underwritten by the Society of Dilettanti, provided lucid and information-laden views of ancient and modern Rome in which the end was not poetic reverie but clear-sighted accuracy (see cat. 149). Wilson while in Italy provided a series of sixty-eight drawings of specific classical sites for the Earl of Dartmouth (see cat. 160). Unlike his own utilitarian sketches, these are highly finished drawings. But as if to distinguish these drawings from the work of the professional topographers, Wilson eschews the pen and wash drawing for black and white chalk on colored paper, media associated with the tradition of old master drawings. He also takes more liberties with the actual topography in the interests of his compositions than a professional topographer would, though this is a matter of degree only. The vaunted accuracy of the topographical draftsman was always subject to manipulation for aesthetic or informational ends.

138

138 John Robert Cozens (1752-1799)

The Bay of Naples from Capodimonte, 1790

Watercolor over graphite on wove paper, laid down on original mount

While the rise of a naturalistic landscape painting in the later part of the eighteenth century and the beginning of the nineteenth can be traced to many sources, one important path of development lies in the creation, largely from the ranks of topographical draftsmen, of a school of watercolor painting, focussed primarily on landscape and given formal embodiment in 1804 with the establishment of the Society of Painters in Water-Colours (Old Water-Colour Society). At the hands of these watercolorists, who now officially designated themselves "painters," the "stained" or "tinted" drawing gave way to a more full-bodied, painterly use of the watercolor medium, while at the same time topographical view-taking ceded ground to naturalistic landscape subjects. If part of the story is the evolution of artists from topographers to landscape painters, another part of the story is the interjection into topography of a more painterly approach and of concerns with light and atmosphere and their expressive potential. At the very moment when Fuseli was delivering his often quoted dismissal of topography as "the tame delineation of a given spot," the notion of topographical truth was expanding to embrace more than the accurate rendering of architectural forms or the features of a view. Indeed, detailed delineation could actually be inimical to the truthful representation of the atmosphere and ambience of a site, a recognition that lies behind the evocative Italian watercolors of John Robert Cozens, based on his visits to Italy in 1776-79 and 1782-83 (see cat. 138).

109 Edward Lear (1812-1888)

Garf Hossayn, 2:30 pm,
15 February 1867 (484)

Pen and brown ink with
watercolor over graphite

109

Cozens's watercolors remain anchored in topographic fact, but detail is sacrificed to mood—a lesson not lost on J. M. W. Turner, who was exposed as a student to Cozens's work. According to that great exponent of stay-at-home landscape painting, John Constable, Cozens was "all poetry." Although there is no indication that Lear knew Cozens's watercolors, the eighteenth-century artist may be considered the fount of that "poetical topography" that Lear professed.

Lear's practice of "penning out" his sketches and adding washes of color stands out from the general practice in watercolor of the nineteenth century. Samuel Prout employed the pen to add detail and definition to his watercolors of Continental architecture, but to most practitioners and aficionados of watercolor art, the use of pen outlines ran counter to prevailing concerns for atmospheric naturalness and would have seemed hopelessly archaic. Indeed, Lear's "penned-out" sketches do seem to be a belated instance of the "stained" or "tinted" drawings of eighteenth-century topography. The resemblance of

188

188 William James Müller (1812-1845)

Near the Caravan Bridge, Smyrna, 1843

Watercolor over graphite

Lear's use of pen and ink and colored washes to that of the topographers of the previous century is suggestive but in the end probably fortuitous. Lear recorded no appreciation or knowledge of his eighteenth-century predecessors. It was not until the later 1850s and 1860s, well after Lear had adopted this particular method of working, that an historical appreciation of the earlier practitioners of the topographical watercolor began to take its place in the public awareness alongside the reverence shown to J.M.W. Turner and the watercolorists of the nineteenth century.[19] For those early topographers, as for Prout later, the pen provided an ideal instrument for conveying architectural detail. But architecture never figured prominently in Lear's art, and it was the boldness of the pen line rather than its delicacy that recommended it to Lear.

The pencil drawing style that Lear took over from Harding offered an almost infinite variety of line and touch and considerable scope and subtlety in atmospheric effects, which Lear sacrificed in adopting the

19 See Scott Wilcox, "Looking Backward: Victorian Perspectives on the Romantic Landscape Watercolor" in *Prospects for the Nation: Recent Essays in British Landscape, 1750-1880*, edited by Michael Rosenthal, Christiana Payne, and Scott Wilcox, *Studies in British Art*, vol. 4 (New Haven and London: Yale University Press, 1997), pp. 307-325.

technique of the "penned-out" sketch. Instead of variety and subtlety, the pen line offered the appearance of decisiveness. Of course one must acknowledge the distinction between the Harding-like drawings of his early years in Italy (carefully crafted objects for consumption) and the later sketches (semi-public documents of the artist's process), but the difference is less that of function than a stripping down of the process of drawing to its essentials. Lear's process of "penning out" enshrined, in a sense ossified, the immediacy of observation. And this immediacy was in part a fiction, for both the pen work and the watercolor were added by Lear after the fact. If Lear never offered these sketches to the public as saleable artistic products, he seems to have been highly self-conscious about their appearance and their role within his artistic process. In this they relate to a broader contemporary appreciation of the sketch and debate about its role vis-à-vis the finished watercolor. The inauguration by the watercolor societies of winter exhibitions of its members' sketches and studies (the Old Society in 1862, the New Society four years later) was a tacit acknowledgement that for all the skill and imagination on display in the highly finished exhibition watercolors of the day, certain qualities of spontaneity and directness had been lost.[20]

William James Müller is an interesting artist in this regard. Like Lear, Müller thought of himself primarily as an oil painter, though his subsequent reputation was based on the brilliance of his watercolors. Unlike Lear, he did not segregate his watercolors into sketches and finished studio works. His watercolors, broad and fluent, were generally completed before the motif in about two hours. It was his policy, which he stated firmly that he had followed with his Lycian watercolors (see cat. 188), not to touch up in the studio.[21]

The degree of hardness that Lear's use of the pen imparts to his sketches echoes a certain crystalline or lapidary quality in his finished watercolors and oils as well. In his insistence on clarity of outline, Lear again aligns himself with an older tradition of topography. In his privileging of form over atmosphere, Lear departs from the example of Turner that he so much admired and comes closer to the Pre-Raphaelite practice of his friend and mentor Holman Hunt. It is well to remember that Lear sometimes referred to himself as a Pre-Raphaelite, even if Lear, temperamentally or perhaps physically given his poor eyesight, was incapable of the preternatural detail of Holman Hunt or J. F. Lewis.

❧

In his pursuit of a career as a topographical artist, Lear was both practical and quixotic, aware of the demands of the marketplace yet never quite able to bring his practice profitably into congruence with those demands. His early illustrated books on Italy were clearly targeted at the audience who had been buying the recent lithographic travel volumes by Prout, Harding, Roberts, and Lewis. Unfortunately the fashion for such volumes would not last much longer, and Lear's later *Journals of a Landscape Painter*, though more personal, are less lavish.

20   See Scott Wilcox and Christopher Newall, *Victorian Landscape Watercolors*, exhibition catalogue (New Haven: Yale Center for British Art, 1992), pp. 43-44.

21   Francis Greenacre and Sheena Stoddard, *W.J. Müller, 1812-1845*, exhibition catalogue (Bristol: Bristol Museums and Art Gallery, 1991), p. 11.

Although he is best known today for his distinctive watercolor sketches, Lear, unlike Prout, Harding, and Lewis (before the later 1850s), did not see himself primarily as an illustrator or draftsman or watercolor painter. He sought to make his reputation and his livelihood as a landscape painter in oils. Despite the advances in public recognition achieved by the watercolor societies, oil painting still occupied a higher rung of public esteem. Roberts's success with his topographical paintings in the Royal Academy exhibitions must have seemed a reasonable model for emulation, and above all loomed the inspiring but daunting example of Turner. Success as a painter was dependent on public recognition in the London exhibitions and on a steady stream of important commissions. Lear's association with Lord Derby at Knowsley had given him access to an important circle of patrons who would support his art throughout his life, but without the public success in the London exhibition scene, that circle of patronage could not expand sufficiently to sustain a career. While Lear enjoyed some success with the paintings he exhibited at the Royal Academy and British Institution in the 1850s, his general experience with public exhibitions was disheartening. By the early 1860s he was railing against the power and corruption of the Royal Academy: "I wish the whole thing were abolished—for as it now is it is disgraceful."[22]

Lear's reliance on aristocratic patronage seemed both outdated and a precarious basis for making a living, as indeed it proved to be. By the mid-nineteenth century artistic careers were made or broken in the public arena. Lear was certainly aware that, in his dependency on private patronage, he was out of step with the times. He wrote of it as "one of the most curious points in my Artistic Career," in a letter of 1877 to one of his patrons, Lord Aberdare. He went on to recount the following exchange: "Said a foolish Artist to me—'you can hardly be ranked as a Painter—because all you have done, or nearly all,—is merely the result of personal consideration, & you are comparatively unknown to the public.' Says I to he,—'that don't at all alter the qualities of my pictures.'"[23] The "foolish Artist" was right in asserting that Lear's painting was relatively unknown to the public. John Ruskin's critical approbation would have meant much to Lear, who wrote to Ruskin in 1883, "Having by your books caused me to use my own eyes in looking at Landscape, from a period dating many years back,"[24] but Ruskin never acknowledged Lear's art in print; his only comment on Lear's work was an appreciative notice of the nonsense verse.[25] When, in his autobiography, William Frith, Lear's fellow student at Sass's School, recalled Lear, it was as the writer of nonsense. His landscape painting appears only as a sad footnote: "Edward Lear, afterwards well known as the author of a child's book called 'A Book of Nonsense,' was one who became an intimate friend of mine, as well as fellow-student. He is still living, I believe, somewhere in Italy. Lear was a man of varied and great accomplishments, a friend of Tennyson's, whose poetry he sang charmingly to music of his own composing. As a landscape-painter he had much merit; but misfortune in the exhibition of his pictures pursued him, as it has done so many others, and at last, I fear, drove him away to try his fortune elsewhere."[26]

22 Letter to Fortescue, March 8, 1862, quoted in Vivien Noakes, *Edward Lear, 1812-1888*, exhibition catalogue (London: Royal Academy, 1985), p. 22.

23 Letter to Lord Aberdare, August 23, 1877, *Selected Letters*, p. 251. In a note, Vivien Noakes suggests that the "foolish artist" might be Lear himself.

24 Letter to John Ruskin, February 16, 1883, *Selected Letters*, p. 262.

25 In a note in the *Pall Mall Gazette* in 1886 Ruskin called *A Book of Nonsense* "inimitable and refreshing, and perfect in rhythm. I really don't know any author to whom I am half so grateful, for my idle self, as Edward Lear." *The Works of John Ruskin*, edited by E. T. Cook and Alexander Wedderburn (London: George Allen, 1903-1912) vol. 34, p. 585.

26 W. P. Frith, *My Autobiography and Reminiscences* (London: Richard Bentley and Son, 1887), vol. 1, p. 44. Lear mentioned the reference to himself in Frith's book in a letter from San Remo on November 10, 1887, *Later Letters*, p. 358.

127 Edward Lear (1812-1888)

A View of the Pine Woods above Cannes, 1869

Watercolor with scraping out
and gum over graphite

127

In addition to his pen and ink and watercolor sketches, which were not for sale, Lear also produced finished watercolors such as the *A View of the Pine Woods above Cannes* (cat. 127) which he did sell to supplement the often disappointing income from his oil paintings. Because of his self-identification as an oil painter, Lear showed little interest in the watercolor societies, only seeking to get into the Old Water-Colour Society — unsuccessfully — after 1870. Lear shied away from the competitive rough and tumble of the great London public exhibitions where an artist could make a name for himself, relying instead on Open Days both in London and abroad, when he set out oils and watercolors in his studio in hope of making sales and garnering commissions from visitors. The number of serious buyers was perforce limited and the process of showing his work personally to often uncomprehending and unsympathetic visitors could itself be torture to the sensitive Lear. To increase sales on these Open Days, Lear mass-produced inexpensive watercolor versions of what he felt to be his more popular compositions. These "tyrants," as Lear called them, have been seen as an unfortunate expedient, harmful to Lear's reputation.[27] But Lear was hardly alone among artists of the period in producing a cheap line of work for ready cash. William James Müller, who did so as well, distinguished between pictures painted "for the world & money" and those painted "for myself" or "for Eternity."[28]

Thomas Hartley Cromek's career offers a number of parallels with Lear's: a lengthy and most productive part of his career spent abroad, a reliance on aristocratic patronage, and disappointment in the more public arena of the London exhibition world. In November 1837, Lear, newly arrived in Italy, received several lessons in watercolors from Cromek, who seven years earlier had made the trip to Italy as a young artist seeking to establish his credentials as a landscape painter. From 1830 until 1849, when the political upheavals forced him to leave (as they precipitated Lear's departure from Italy the previous year), Cromek was based in Florence and Rome. He traveled widely in the Italian peninsula, and in 1834 he

27 For Lear's "tyrants," see Noakes 1985, pp. 39-40, and Noakes 1991, pp. 80-81.

28 Greenacre and Stoddard, p. 12.

164

164 Thomas Hartley Cromek (1809-1873)

The Parthenon, c. 1834

Watercolor over graphite

toured Greece and Albania and would have gone on to the Holy Land and Egypt (a very Lear-like itinerary) had he not been deterred by reports of plague.[29]

In Italy Cromek enjoyed considerable success giving drawing lessons and selling his watercolors to visiting nobility. During a visit to England in 1843, he showed his drawings to Victoria and Albert, and two were purchased for the Royal Collection. However, Cromek's attempts to reach a wider audience through the professional organizations and exhibitions in London met with little success. After unsuccessful bids to be elected to the Old Water-Colour Society in 1837 and 1850, he was elected associate of the New Watercolour Society in 1850, but of the eight drawings he exhibited at the New Society in 1851, not one was sold. He was similarly unsuccessful in selling the watercolors he sent to the Royal Academy exhibitions in 1835 and 1850, and, from an exhibition of his own work that he organized in Manchester in 1854, he sold only one small drawing. His years back in England after 1849, characterized by lack of recognition and consequent financial hardship, suggest even more strikingly than Lear's experience the

29 *Thomas Hartley Cromek: A Classical Vision*, exhibition catalogue (Leeds: The Harewood House Trust, 1999), p. 11.

193

185

193 David Roberts (1796-1864)

The Great Temple of Amon Karnak, the Hypostyle Hall, 1838

Watercolor and gouache with scratching out over graphite on beige wove paper

limits of aristocratic patronage in sustaining a career as a topographical painter in the nineteenth century and the difficulties in coping with the changing taste of a broader public.

Neither Cromek nor Lear were in step with fashions in topographical art. By the 1850s, Cromek's watercolors must have seemed austere, lacking the verve of William Callow and J. D. Harding, the sentiment and picturesque appeal of Thomas Miles Richardson, Junior, and William Leighton Leitch, or the Pre-Raphaelite intensity of William Holman Hunt and Thomas Seddon. The glowing, light-drenched Middle Eastern watercolors of John Frederick Lewis were generating excitement in the exhibitions of the Society of Painters in Water-Colours, but these were genre rather than strictly topographical subjects. Compared with the vivid watercolors of Lewis, Holman Hunt and Seddon, the Middle Eastern views of David Roberts, whether in watercolors, lithographs or oils, were dull and old-fashioned. If Roberts's *Egypt and the Holy Land* marked the highpoint of the vogue for lavish lithographic travel books, it also marked the beginning of the end for such publications. Following the events of the Indian Uprising in

174

185 John Frederick Lewis (1805-1876)

The Ramesseum at Thebes c. 1850?

Watercolor and gouache over graphite
on beige wove paper

174 Francis Frith (1822-1898)

Lower Egypt, Thebes, and the Pyramids
London: William MacKenzie, 1862

Shown: *Valley of the Nile from the
Quarries of Toura*
Albumen print from wet collodion negative

Beinecke Rare Book and Manuscript
Library

1857, William Day of the major lithographic firm Day and Son commissioned William Simpson to create drawings for a massive volume on India, with which he hoped to revive the flagging fortunes of his business. The model was Roberts's *Egypt and the Holy Land*, for which Day and Son had been the printer (the publisher was F. G. Moon). After Simpson had spent almost two and a half years traveling in India and another three to four years working up his sketches into two hundred and fifty finished watercolors, Day and Son went bankrupt in 1867 before the projected volume could be completed. Simpson subsequently made his living as a travel artist of a different sort, working as an artist correspondent for the *Illustrated London News*.

By the late 1850s the topographical draftsman and illustrator had a potent competitor in the photographer. Between 1856 and 1859, Francis Frith made three tours of Egypt and the Holy Land. The resulting photographs, published in several different formats (see cat. 173 and 174) were, according to *The Times*, "far beyond anything that is in the power of the most accomplished artist to transfer to his canvas."[30]

30 Quoted in Mark Haworth-Booth, ed., *Golden Age of British Photography, 1839-1900*, exhibition catalogue (London: Victoria and Albert Museum, 1984), p. 83.

177 John Fulleylove (1845-1908)

The Castalian Spring, Delphi, c. 1895

Watercolor over graphite
with scraping out

177

In 1859 Frith opened a photographic printing establishment which assembled a vast archive of topographical views. Francis Bedford, who had launched his photographic career with photographs of David Roberts's lithographs at the Photographic Society of London's first exhibition in 1853, provided photographic documentation of the Prince of Wales's tour of the Near East in 1862 (cat. 162). The photograph seemed to offer by its very nature that assurance of accuracy and factuality on which the topographical enterprise was built, whereas the topographical artist continually had to struggle to convince his audience of that same veracity of representation. Some topographical draftsmen and painters found photography a useful tool. Lear purchased a "photographic machine" in 1856, which he hoped would "be of great service to me in copying plants, & in many things which distance, limited time, heat, etc. would prevent my getting." Although he continued to express interest in taking his own photographs for reference, he does not seem to have made it a practice. He did, however, purchase commercial photographs in Crete in 1864 and in India in 1873.[31] But photography inevitably shifted the position of other topographical art either towards reportage (until the technology allowed photography to supplant wood-engraving as the medium of the illustrated weekly) or towards a more purely aesthetic stance to the subject matter, as is evident in the watercolor illustrations of John Fulleylove (see cat. 175-177), as travel art entered the twentieth century.

31 Noakes 1991, p. 11

℘

The successful marketing of the artist traveler to a popular audience rested on a paradox. In his pursuit of the exotic, in his quest to lay before a western audience what had previously been hidden from their gaze, the artist heroically endured hardship, overcame obstacles, faced down dangers. He was celebrated (or at least promoted) as a hero, and his art carried the aura of his heroism.[32] Yet the art had value as the accurate record of a place or people, and to that extent it should not be distorted by the artist's personality. He must be the passive recorder, the transparent eye. The photographer Francis Frith enjoyed an advantage in this regard. Much could be made of his heroic efforts carting his cameras and glass plate negatives across the desert, while at the same time the medium itself seemed to insure against the possibility of the artist's manipulation or falsification of the image.

32 The celebration of the travel artist (invariably male) as hero raises the issue of gender. The ranks of travel writers included many notable women from Lady Mary Wortley Montagu to Thomasina Campbell, whom Lear met in Corsica; however, travel artists, at least professional travel artists, seem to have been overwhelmingly male. Note should be made of amateurs, such as Emily Eden, whose *Portraits of the Princes and People of India*, lithographed by L. Dickinson in 1844, enjoyed considerable success.

An example of the presentation, or self-presentation, of the artist traveler as hero comes in the brief memoir by William James Müller of an adventure in Egypt, published in the *Art-Union* after his death, with the editorial note that it was "a striking record of one of the many perils the accomplished writer underwent in his search after knowledge." Müller begins his account, "I had revelled in temples (pardon the expression), I had lived in tombs, I had boiled my tea-kettle with mummies' bones, descended into labyrinths of passages — poking up from their long hidden places, birds and beasts. In short, I had become artist, naturalist, and half Arab. I had ridden a camel, and I had shot at — but never *killed* — a crocodile."[33]

33 William James Müller, "Visit to the Crocodile Caves," *Art-Union*, March 1846, p. 79

The adoption by an artist of the lifestyle and costume of the people whose landscape he was recording served to enhance both the perception of the artist as adventurer and his seriousness as an accurate observer. While few artists "went native," the portrayal of artists such as Müller, Roberts, and Frith in native garb, though in many instances little more than play-acting, lent an air of exoticism to the artist himself and suggested a knowledge of the culture based on personal identification with it and immersion in it. John Frederick Lewis's ten year stay in Cairo is an instance of an artist seriously adopting the attributes

84 Edward Lear (1812-1888)

Dendour, 2:15 pm, 31 January 1867 (298)

Pen and brown ink with watercolor
and gouache over graphite
on gray wove paper

84

34 Holman Hunt, vol. 1, p. 332. Hunt continued that
Lear was "at the same time the most indomitable
being in encountering danger and hardship. Nothing
daunted him, and yet no one could be more fearful
than he of certain difficulties he had to face as the
fixed conditions of travelling."

35 Letter to Fortescue, March 9, 1858, *Letters*, p. 92.

36 Letter to Lady Waldegrave, May 27, 1858, *Letters*,
pp.101-103.

of a foreign culture, in a way reminiscent of the noted Egyptologist Edward William Lane, whose own much longer stay in Egypt overlapped with Lewis's. Although Lear spent much of his life in various locations in the Mediterranean, he seems to have always been the eccentric English artist abroad.

Lear made an unlikely hero. With his poor eyesight, his asthma, and his epilepsy, he scarcely cut a dashing figure. Though he was a large and somewhat imposing man, Holman Hunt described him as "uncombative as a tender girl."[34] Nevertheless, he showed a stoical determination in the pursuit of his topographical art, despite ailments and adversity, that is quietly heroic. He did not flinch from discomfort or even danger. Before his visit to Palestine in 1858, Lear, who had "never touched firearms in all my days," was trained in the use of a revolver by his friend Franklin Lushington because "you can't do work at the Dead Sea without them."[35] Although Lear never availed himself of the pistol that Lushington had given him, the trip was not free of threatening incident. As he reported in a letter to Lady Waldegrave:

> The country is in such a state that many places can only be visited at the risk of robbery &c., even if the traveller goes over the ground as rapidly as possibly, so travelling,— he may escape outrage, but with me, that mode of progress is useless: — I must stop and for a considerable time, so that it is not easy to escape those odious Arabs. The whole plain of Eisdroelon for instance swarms with them, & they attack all passengers.... Of my own mishaps at Petra you perhaps have heard; how about 200 of them came down on me, and every-thing which could be divided they took. My watch they returned to me, but all money, handkerchiefs, knives, &c., &c., were confiscated.[36]

However willing Lear was to suffer discomfort, indignity, even physical danger in the course of travel, and despite the value attached to views of little known and seldom depicted countries, he was by no means an explorer or a pioneering view-taker. Although he could claim that certain of his sketches and

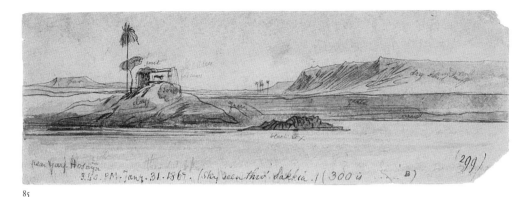

85

85 Edward Lear (1812–1888)

Near Garf Hossayn, 3:40 pm,
31 January 1867 (299)

Pen and brown ink with watercolor
over graphite

published illustrations presented to the British public sites that were new to them, he was almost always following in the footsteps of earlier British travelers whose writings or drawings had already been published. By the time of Lear's first trip to Egypt in 1849, a decade had elapsed since the visits of Roberts and Müller. The first part of Roberts's *Egypt and Nubia* had appeared three years before. And it was not just other intrepid artist travelers and Egyptologists who had preceded Lear. Murray had published his first guidebook to Egypt in 1847, and, though Thomas Cook's first tour to Egypt did not take place until 1869, European and even North American tourists were already a well-established presence. The absence of westerners, or of people altogether, often gives Lear's drawings a sense of isolation, of Lear on his own in unknown country. Yet comments on his trip up the Nile in 1867, so well represented in this exhibition (cat. 60–123), make clear that he was far from the only western visitor: "An 'American' or Montreal cousin was with me above Luxor, but he was a fearful bore; of whom it is only necessary to say that he whistled all day aloud — & that he was 'disappointed' in Abou Simbel. You cannot imagine the extent of the American element in travel here! They are as 25 to one English. They go about in dozens & scores — one dragoman to so many — & are a fearful race mostly."[37] Lear sounds a note, here in private correspondence, that would become a refrain of travel writing in the age of the Cook's Tour: the disdain for the tourist on the part of the serious traveler.

There is no doubting Lear's seriousness, his indefatigable dedication to recording the landscape of the Mediterranean. Yet he could contrast himself with other more "serious" and more stalwart travelers, creating a consciously anti-heroic image. From Corsica in 1868, he wrote to Emily Tennyson about one such traveler: "A Miss Campbell — a vast & manlike maiden — has been here for months with her singularly ugly female servt — & she roars & raves about Corsica, — goes hither & thither, & is bringing out a book about it. I could well have wished to do the same, could I manage to see the whole place —

37 Letter to Lady Waldegrave, March 9, 1867, *Selected Letters*, p. 209.

86 Edward Lear (1812-1888)

Near Mereeh or Garf Hossayn, 4:00 pm, 31 January 1867 (302)

Pen and brown ink with watercolor and gouache over graphite on gray wove paper

86

38 Letter to Emily Tennyson, May 6, 1868, *Selected Letters*, p. 212.

but I am sorry to say my servant Giorgio has just got an attack of fever — & I can't manage alone, as it is a very rough country to travel in, except for such strong folk as Miss Campbell. It will be a considerable bore to have made the voyage & spent a lot of tin for nothing."[38] Thomasina M. A. E. Campbell did bring out her *Notes on the Island of Corsica in 1868, Dedicated to those in search of Health and Enjoyment* later that year with a frontispiece based on a drawing by Lear. Lear published his *Journal of a Landscape Painter in Corsica* (cat. 129) in 1870.

In the preface to that volume, Lear makes a statement that suggests both the purposive nature as well as the element of chance in his travels: "I passed last winter at Cannes, intending to return early in the spring to Palestine, for the purpose of completing drawings and journals for a work already partly advanced; but circumstances having prevented me from carrying out this plan, I decided on going to Corsica, rather perhaps on account of its being a place near at hand and easily reached, than from any distinct impression as to the nature of the country, or from any particular interest in its history, inhabitants, or scenery."[39] In part Lear is setting up the narrative structure for the journal: a movement from ignorance of Corsica and an initial distaste for the country to an eventual appreciation of its real beauties. But in acknowledging that offhand nature of his decision to make a trip to Corsica, Lear admits into his topographical project the role of happenstance and contingency. From his travels to Greece and Egypt in 1848-49 to the Indian tour of 1873-74, Lear's movements were most frequently the result of invitations from friends and acquaintances.

39 Edward Lear, *Journal of a Landscape Painter in Corsica* (London: Robert John Bush, 1870), p. vii.

In the careers of the most adventurous and the most systematic of travel artists, there is a comparable element of contingency. Lear made the most of his opportunities. In his attempts "to topographize and topographize all the journeyings of my life," he worked tirelessly to transmute personal experience into something of general and lasting value.

Lear's description of himself as "a painter of poetical topography" implies a prosaic topography from which he sought to differentiate his own painting. Poetry was often invoked by artists and critics of the nineteenth century in connection with landscape painting either to praise some ineffable quality of mind or perception or to draw attention to a perceived deficiency of feeling or imagination. As applied to the visual arts, poetry was a capacious and amorphous concept. One critic's poetry could be another's sentimentality and picturesque formula.

A certain theatricality in David Roberts's paintings and drawings betrays his origins as a scene painter. Yet this aspect of Roberts's work went unnoted by John Ruskin, who characterized his work as "true portraiture of scenes of historical and religious interest." For Ruskin, Roberts, though "utterly destitute of imagination," fulfilled a role, important for his time, as "a kind of grey mirror" who "with unwearied industry, both in Egypt and Spain, brought home records of which the value is now forgotten in the perfect detail of photography."[40]

40   *Praeterita*, in *Works*, vol. 35, pp. 262 and 404.

Perhaps the most cogent and sustained consideration of an imaginative or poetical topography is Ruskin's chapter "Of Turnerian Topography" in Volume IV of *Modern Painters,* published in 1856. Following his division of art into the simple ("historical") and the imaginative ("poetical") relation of fact, he makes the distinction in landscape between simple topography and Turnerian topography. Ruskin argues for the value of simple topography, writing that "the duty of every painter at present, who has not much invention, is to take subjects of which the portraiture will be precious in after times."[41] At the same time he establishes a topographical hierarchy, the upper rung of which, occupied by Turner alone, is achievable only through genius, a sort of alchemy or "mental chemistry," to use Ruskin's words, by which memories and associations are transmuted, without conscious manipulation by the artist, into images which are more truthful than simple factual representations. Lifetimes of memory are stored up in the mind of the Turnerian topographer "as in vast warehouses." "Over all this unindexed and immeasurable mass of treasure, the imagination brooding and wandering, but dream-gifted, so as to summon at any moment exactly such groups of ideas as shall justly fit each other: this I conceive to be the real nature of the imaginative mind."[42] In comparison, mere scientific truth, which is the most that the general run of artists can hope to achieve, is "truth of the husk and surface, hard and shallow; and only the imaginative truth is precious."[43]

41   *Works*, vol. 6, p. 31.

42   Ibid., p. 42.
43   Ibid., pp. 44-45.

Ruskin, to the extent that he was aware of Lear's landscape art, did not deem it worthy of note. Judged by Ruskin's high standard of "Turnerian topography," Lear falls short. And Lear was certainly aware of his own shortcomings when measured against the achievements of Turner. In his diary in 1877 he wrote: "Depressed enough already—the glory & beauty of the Turners depressed me still more."[44] Should we deny to Lear the vein of poetry that he claimed for his topographical painting?

44   Diary, August 1, 1877, Noakes, 1985, p. 20.

If, from the welter of meanings attached to poetry as a term of art criticism in the nineteenth century, we can extract any meaning for topographical art, it is, perhaps, first, that poetry in the travel artist arises from an individual sensibility responding to and making sense of foreign subject matter. This is, in essence, Ruskin's Turnerian topography, though made more inclusive. And, secondly, that poetical topography arises from some structuring principle that elevates the image beyond the simple record of appearance. The structuring principle of much travel art lay in the contrast of the greatness of past civilizations and the degraded state of their present-day successors, or in the contrast of the familiarity of the classical past, the common coin of western civilization, with the unfamiliarity, the exoticism, of the present eastern cultures. Each partakes of a measure of xenophobia. While Lear's paintings and drawings indulge the taste for the exotic, the structuring principle is different, reflecting Lear's lack of interest in architecture and his uneasiness about his abilities as a figure draftsman. In Lear's art, as in his writings, one finds bemusement and at times condescension, but not the racial antipathy and cultural superiority that seem to color much of the work of his predecessors and contemporaries. For Lear, the remains of ancient civilizations, be they Greek, Roman, or Egyptian, are subsumed into the landscape. Natural features, monuments of antiquity, present inhabitants, all exist within the eternal processes of nature, all recorded with an equal sense of wonder and detachment.

The overarching principle of Lear's art, though not articulated as such, comes close to what might be termed the scientific sublime of the American landscape painter Frederic Edwin Church. Church's epic canvases *Heart of the Andes,* 1859 (Metropolitan Museum of Art, New York), *Cotopaxi,* 1862 (Detroit Institute of Arts), and *Chimborazo,* 1864 (Huntington Library, San Marino), all exhibited with great success in London in the 1860s, represent natural history illustration elevated to the level of grand manner history painting. Given Lear's background, he must have found such an approach particularly sympathetic, and, indeed, Lear was an admirer of Church's work, writing in 1880: "I consider [him] the greatest Landscape Painter after Turner; — & one of his works, 'The Heart of the Andes' hangs always before me." For Lear, as for Church, landscape painting consisted of natural history filtered through the artistic sensibility. When Lear went on to make the case for Church's significance, he did so in terms that could equally apply to his own life's work and the public reaction to it: "I have heard Church's works decried as wanting in certain technical qualities, & conditions of art: — yet he is not the greatest Orator — it seems to me, — who can speak with perfect fluency & charm of rhetoric on one or two subjects, — but rather he who with less power of eloquence or popular persuasiveness can bring home to the hearts & minds of his audience convictions on a multitude of different subjects with unfailing force. The painter who all his life paints Surrey woodlands or English coast scenes arrives at a perfection in what he aims at, & is a delight & a benefactor; — but he who can portray Arctic scenes, South American magnificences & endless other distinctly various phases of nature, is far more a delight & a far greater benefactor to his art & his country."[45] In oil paintings like the *Kangchenjunga from Darjeeling* (cat. 130), in which his debt to the landscapes of Church is most apparent, in his finished watercolors and the innumerable watercolor and pen and ink sketches, and in his published travel books (not to mention the journals that remained unpublished in his lifetime but are now in print),[46] Lear has provided a greater delight and benefaction than he could ever have anticipated.

45 Letter to James Fields, January 18, 1880, Noakes 1985, p. 20.

46 These include *Edward Lear's Indian Journal: Watercolours and Extracts from the Diary of Edward Lear 1873-1875,* edited by Ray Murphy (London: Jarrolds, 1953); *Edward Lear: The Cretan Journal,* edited by Rowena Fowler (Athens and Dedham: Denise Harvey and Co., 1984); *Edward Lear: The Corfu Years: A Chronicle Presented through His Letters and Journals,* edited by Philip Sherrard (Athens and Dedham: Denise Harvey and Co., 1988); and *Edward Lear in the Levant: Travels in Albania, Greece, and Turkey in Europe 1848-1849,* edited by Susan Hyman (London: John Murray, 1988).

Catalogue

PART ONE: Edward Lear

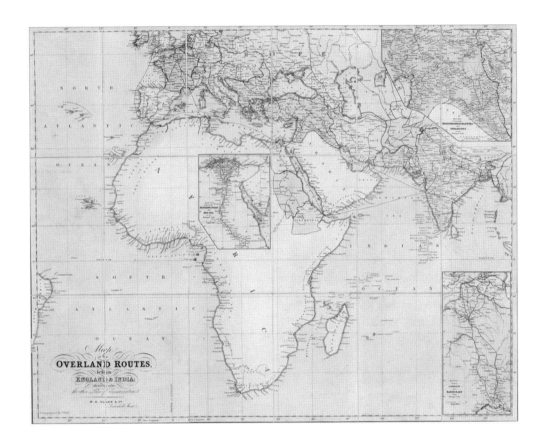

The catalogue is in two parts: the first devoted to Edward Lear, the second to other British artist travelers working in the Mediterranean and India from the 1750s to the 1890s. In the Lear section, works are arranged in chronological order, although strict chronology is broken in a few instances to group together related material. Unless otherwise indicated, works are the gift of Donald C. Gallup, Yale, 1934, Ph.D., 1939.

The second section is divided into two chronological groupings, one for the eighteenth century and one for the nineteenth, within which the artists are ordered alphabetically. Unless otherwise indicated, the works in this section are from the Paul Mellon Collection.

All works for which the support is not specified are on white or off-white wove paper. All books and manuscripts are from the Center's Department of Rare Books and Archives unless otherwise noted.

Authors of the entries are identified by their initials: Eva Bowerman (EB), Clay Dean (CD), Morna O'Neill (MO), Stephen Vella (SV), and Emily Weeks (EW). All unsigned entries are by Scott Wilcox.

1 *Platycercus Brownii (Brown's Parrakeet),*
from *Illustrations of the Family
of Psittacidae, or Parrots,* 1832

Hand-colored lithograph
20 ¼ x 13 ⅜ in. (51.4 x 34 cm)

Printed inscription on branch: *E. Lear*;
at bottom center: PLATYCERUS BROWNII /
Brown's Parrakeet; lower left: E. LEAR DEL ET
LITH; lower right: *Printed by C. Hullmandel*

B 1997.7.376

By his own account, Lear began to earn a
living as a draftsman in 1827. Within three
years he gained permission from the
Zoological Society of London to draw their
parrots and began to publish by subscription
his *Illustrations of the Family of Psittacidae, or
Parrots.* Working with the noted lithographer
Charles Hullmandel, Lear produced a series
of hand-colored lithographic images of parrots,
mostly life-size, that were much admired
by ornithologists. However, not all his sub-
scribers were prompt in making payment,
and in 1832 he brought the series to a premature
close with the twelfth part; he had intended
another two. On the basis of his illustrations
of parrots, Lear was elected an Associate of
the Linnean Society and gained work in natural history illustration from the ornithologist
John Gould and the President of the London
Zoological Society, Lord Stanley, who would
become one of Lear's most important patrons.

PLATYCERCUS BROWNII.

Brown's Parrakeet.

1

2

2 *A Weasel*, 1832

Watercolor with pen and brown ink,
with white gouache and gum over graphite
7 ½ x 11 ⅛ in. (19.1 x 28.3 cm)

Signed and dated bottom center: *E. Lear
del. / August. 29th. 1832*; inscribed verso:
Mustela Putorius. Female. August. 29. 1832.

Paul Mellon Collection
B 1975.4.1318

As early as 1831 Lear was working in the
menagerie of Knowsley Hall, drawing animals at the invitation of Lord Stanley, who
would become the 13th Earl of Derby in 1834.
Lear continued to produce natural history
drawings for Lord Derby until 1837, although
he complained of the strain such work placed
on his deteriorating eye-sight, which he gave
as one of his reasons for switching from natural history to landscape. In 1846 Lord Derby
published a selection of Lear's watercolors
under the title *Gleanings from the Menagerie
and Aviary at Knowsley Hall.*

3 *Peppering*, 3 October 1834

Graphite

4 ⅜ x 6 ½ in. (11.1 x 16.5 cm)

Inscribed lower left: *Peppering. / Oct. 3. 1834*

B 1997.7.9

4 *Peppering*, 3 October 1834

Graphite

4 ½ x 6 ½ in. (11.4 x 16.5 cm)

Inscribed lower left: *Peppering. / Oct. 3. 1834*

B 1997.7.10

These, amongst the earliest of Lear's landscape drawings, are two pages of a sketchbook. Peppering House, near Arundel in Sussex, was the home of Fanny Drewitt, a childhood friend of Lear. Lear's earliest nonsense verse was done for the Drewitt family.

3

4

5

5 *Parham*, 13 October 1834

Graphite with white gouache
on gray wove paper
10 ⅜ x 6 ¹³⁄₁₆ in. (26 x 17.1 cm)

Inscribed lower right: *Oct. 13. 1834 / Parham*

B 1997.7.12

6 *North Stoke*, 21 October 1834

Graphite with white gouache
on gray wove paper
10 x 13 ⅞ in. (25.4 x 35.2 cm)

Inscribed bottom center: *North Stoke. /
Oct. 21. 1834.*

B 1997.7.14

Lear's studies of trees in the autumn of 1834
are strikingly similar to J. D. Harding's lithographic illustrations in his *Elementary Art; or,
The Use of the Lead Pencil Advocated and
Explained,* which was published that same
year. Harding included an extended series of
exercises in the delineation of trees, which, as
Lear moved from the exactitude of natural
history draftsmanship to the broader practice
of landscape, provided a useful guide. Harding
noted that trees "cannot, in their forms, be
copied with rigid accuracy" but must be
represented by the "application of the means
of Art."[1] Lear adopted Harding's "art," or
conventions of drawing, as he did Harding's
recommended media: graphite on gray paper
with highlights in white gouache. This
Harding-like approach to drawing remained
central to Lear's landscape art for more than
a decade.

1   J. D. Harding's *Elementary Art; or, The Use of the Lead
Pencil Advocated and Explained* (London: Charles
Tilt, 1834), p. 33.

6

7

7 *Knowsley Hall*, 28 October 1834

Graphite on heavy beige wove paper
10 ⅝ x 15 in. (27.0 x 38.1 cm)

Dated lower right: *28 Oct*;
with other notations

B 1997.7.15

Knowsley Hall, near Liverpool, was the home of the Earl of Derby. Lear first came to Knowsley in 1831 to draw birds and animals in the menagerie there. He became a great favorite of the family, and throughout his life he continued to visit and work at Knowsley on his periodic returns to England. In January 1883, the 15th Earl of Derby, grandson of Lear's great early patron, wrote to Lear: "Come over this spring and bring a room full of work with you. There is space still at Knowsley for a few more of your drawings, though I have a pretty good stock already."[1] But by that date Lear had made his last visit to England.

1 Quoted in Noakes 1968, p. 297.

The Lake District, 1836

1   Letter to John Gould, October 31, 1836,
    Selected Letters, p. 23.

Lear made a walking tour of the Lake District from the middle of August to mid-October 1836. After his return to Knowsley, he wrote to John Gould: "Really it is impossible to tell you *how, & how enormously* I have enjoyed the whole Autumn. The counties of Cumberland & Westmorland are superb indeed, & tho' the weather has been miserable, yet I have contrived to walk pretty well over the whole ground, & to sketch a good deal besides. I hope too, I have improved somewhat—(hard if I haven't after slaving as I have done) but you will judge when I get back."[1]

8   *Furness Abbey East*, 29 August 1836

Graphite with white gouache
on gray wove paper
7 ⅞ x 12 in. (20 x 30.5 cm)

Inscribed lower left: *Furness Abbey. East /
29 Aug. 1836.*

B 1997.7.23

8

9

10

9 *Calder Abbey*, 12 September 1836

Graphite with stump and white gouache
on gray wove paper
9 ⅛ x 13 ⅛ in. (23.2 x 33.3 cm)

Inscribed lower left: *Calder Abbey /
September. 12. 1836*

B 1997.7.24

10 *Yewbarrow, Wastwater*, 16 September 1836

Graphite with stump and white gouache
on gray wove paper
6 ¾ x 10 ⅛ in. (17.1 x 25.7 cm)

Inscribed lower right: *Yewbarrow. Wastwater. /
16 September 1836 / 17*; with other notations

B 1997.7.25

11 *Derwentwater*, [21? September 1836]

Graphite with stump and white gouache
on gray wove paper
6 ⁹⁄₁₆ x 10 in. (16.7 x 25.6 cm)

Inscribed lower left: *Derwentw*[cut off]

B 1997.7.26

12 *Derwentwater*, [21? September 1836]

Graphite with stump and white gouache
on gray wove paper
6 ⅝ x 10 in. (16.8 x 25.4 cm)

Inscribed lower left: *Derwent Water Septr
1836*; lower right: *36*

B 1997.7.27

13 *Ullswater*, 14 Oct. 1836
SEE PAGE 15

Graphite with stump and white gouache
on gray wove paper
6 ⅝ x 9 ⅞ in. (16.8 x 25.1 cm)

Inscribed lower right: *Ullswater / 14 Oct*

B 1997.7.32

11

12

With financial backing from Lord Derby and Robert Hornby, Lear set out for Italy in the summer of 1837. He spent much time in September and October in the Italian Lakes and November in Florence, arriving in Rome early in December. For most of the next ten years, Lear wintered in Rome and toured other parts of Italy in the summers.

14

14 *St. Giulio, Orta,* 26 September 1837

Graphite with stump and
white gouache on brown wove paper
10 x 14 ¼ in. (25.4 x 36.2 cm) corners cut

Inscribed lower left: *St. Guilio. Orta / 26. Sept. 1837*; with other notations

B 1997.7.35

Lear employed his Harding-derived style, in graphite with stump and white gouache on colored paper, in drawings of varying degrees of finish. This precisely dated drawing with other notations was presumably done on the spot or shortly thereafter. A very similar but more finished version, signed and dated 1839, is in the British Museum.[1]

1 See Noakes 1985, p. 98.

15 *Genezzano*, 17 May 1838

Graphite with stump and white
gouache on gray wove paper
10 x 14 in. (25.4 x 35.6 cm) corners cut

Inscribed lower right: *Genezzano /
17. May. 1838*

B 1997.7.38

16 *Corpo di Cava*, 28 June 1838
SEE PAGE 16

Oil on gray wove paper
14 ⅛ x 9 ¾ in. (35.9 x 24.8 cm)

Inscribed lower left: *Corpo di Cava /
28. June. 1838*

B 1997.7.41

17 *La Cava*, 19 July 1838

Graphite on gray wove paper
14 x 10 in. (35.6 x 25.4 cm)

Inscribed lower right: *La Cava /
19. July 1838*

B 1997.7.39

15

17

18

19

18   *La Cava*, 20 July 1838

Graphite on gray wove paper

10 x 13 ⅞ in. (25.6 x 35.2 cm)

Inscribed lower left: *La Cava / July. 20. 1838*

B 1997.7.40

19   *Sorrento*, 2 August 1838

Graphite on gray wove paper

6 ¾ x 10 ⅛ in. (17.1 x 25.7 cm)

Inscribed lower right: *Sorrento. / 2. August. 1838*; with other notations

B 1997.7.43

In May 1838 Lear, in company with his fellow artist Thomas Uwins, traveled to the Bay of Naples. To John Gould, Lear wrote: "Naples does not please me as a city, altho' no other word but Paradise can be used to express the beauty of its environs, which are unlike any earthy scene beside:—but the town itself is all noise, horror—dirt, heat—& abomination—& I hate it."[1] After a few days in Naples, Lear and Uwins retreated to the village of Corpo di Cava, southeast of Naples. There Lear produced his first oil paintings, small sketches of trees and vegetation, presumably painted on the spot (cat. 16). The drawings in emphatic pencil outline (cat. 17 and 18) suggest that he may also have been experimenting with an optical device such as a camera lucida.

[1] Letter to John Gould, October 17, 1839, *Selected Letters*, p. 47.

20 *Segni*, 6 October 1838

Black chalk with stump and white gouache
on gray wove paper
10 x 13 ⅝ in. (25.4 x 34.6 cm) corners cut

Inscribed lower right: *Segni. / 6. Octobr 1838*

B 1997.7.45

21 *Temple of Venus and Rome, Rome*, 1840

Oil on paper laid down on cardboard
9 ⅝ x 13 ⅜ in. (24.4 x 34 cm)

Paul Mellon Fund

B 1980.33

Like the oil sketches from Corpo di Cava,
this small oil seems to have been painted on
the spot. Such a work places Lear within a
tradition of plein-air sketching in oils by foreign artists in Italy that stretches from Pierre-
Henri de Valenciennes and Thomas Jones in
the eighteenth century.[1] The ruins of the
Temple of Venus and Rome, built by the
Emperor Hadrian, stand in the eastern end
of the Forum. To the right rises the medieval
bell tower of the church of Santa Francesca
Romana. An eighteenth-century watercolor
of the site by William Pars is also in the exhibition (cat. 149).

1 This connection was noted by Mary Anne Stevens in
Noakes 1985, p.139. The tradition is explored in
Philip Conisbee, et al., *In the Light of Italy: Corot
and Early Open-Air Painting*, exhibition catalogue
(Washington: National Gallery of Art, 1996).

20

21

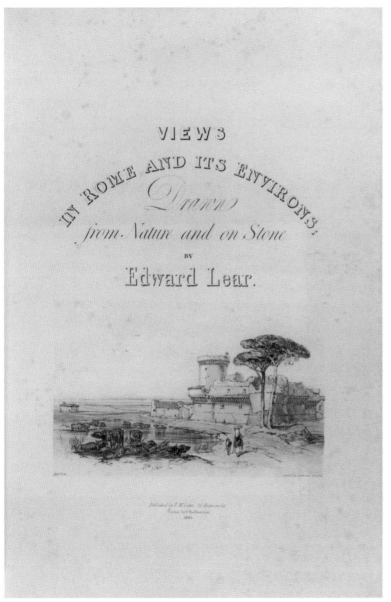

22

22 *Views in Rome and its Environs;*
Drawn from Nature and on Stone
London: T. McLean, 1841

Shown: Title page
Lithograph

Paul Mellon Collection

When Lear returned to England for a visit in the summer and autumn of 1841, he had in mind to publish a series of lithographs based on his Italian drawings to cover expenses. In the late summer, he was working at Knowsley on the lithographic stones for *Views in Rome and its Environs*, his first travel book. The twenty-five lithographs were printed by Charles Hullmandel, who had previously published Lear's lithographs of parrots as well as many of the popular lithographic volumes by travel artists such as Prout, Harding, Roberts, and Lewis.

23 *Valmontone,* from *Views in Rome and its Environs,* 1841
SEE PAGE 15

Lithograph
Image: 9 ½ x 15 in. (23.5 x 37.5 cm)

Printed inscription lower left: *VALMONTONE*; lower right: *EDWARD LEAR DEL ET LITH.* Inscribed in pencil below image lower left: *(25 miles from Rome) town & palace of Doria family*

B 1997.7.389

24 *Campagna of Rome from Villa Mattei,* from *Views in Rome and its Environs,* 1841
SEE PAGE 22

Lithograph
Image: 9 ⅞ x 17 in.

Printed inscription lower left: *CAMPAGNA OF ROME FROM VILLA MATTEI;* lower right: *EDWARD LEAR DEL ET LITH.*

B 1997.7.390

25 *Rome from Via della Porta, San Paolo,* from *Views in Rome and its Environs,* 1841

Lithograph
Image: 9 ⅜ x 16 ¾ in. (23.3 x 42.5 cm)

Printed inscription lower left: *ROME FROM VIA DELLA PORTA SAN PAOLO;* lower right: *EDWARD LEAR DEL ET LITH.*

B 1997.7.391

26 *Isola di Sora,* 31 Mar. 1842

Graphite with stump on gray wove paper
6 ⅝ x 10 ⅛ in. (16.8 x 25.7 cm)

Inscribed lower right: *Isola di Sora / 31. March 1842;* with other notations

B 1997.7.47

As Donald Gallup has pointed out, Lear indicated in a letter to Lord Derby that he was in Sicily in March 1842, and Sora is on the mainland between Rome and Naples.[1] The drawing seems to reflect Lear's style at the time, and the inscriptions seem to be in his hand. It would appear to be a drawing done on the spot, but, as Lear did return to his sketches, perhaps he added the place and date later, incorrectly recalling when he had visited Sora.

1 Gallup, p. 85. The letter to Lord Derby, dated June 5, 1842, is published in *Selected Letters,* pp. 53-60.

25

26

27

28

27 *A Study of Ferns, Civitella*, 1842

Oil on gray wove paper

6 ¼ x 7 ⅝ in. (15.9 x 19.4 cm)

Inscribed lower left: *Civitella. / Octr. 15. 1842.*

Paul Mellon Collection

B 1981.25.416

28 *Between Olevano and Civitella*, 1842

Oil on canvas

10 ½ x 14 ½ in. (26.7 x 36.8 cm)

Signed and dated lower right: *E. Lear 1842*

B 1997.7.5

Lear credited his introduction to the hill towns of Civitella and Olevano to Penry Williams, an English painter and longtime resident in Rome with whom Lear became friends. Lear included views of both Olevano and Civitella in *Views in Rome and its Environs*. Lear painted a number of variants of this composition, including a grand painting (50 x 76 inches) in 1847 titled *Civitella di Subiaco* (The Clothworkers' Company).[1]

1 See Noakes 1985, p.140.

29 *Landscape with Goatherd*, c. 1842

Oil on canvas
10 ½ x 14 ½ in. (26.7 x 36.8 cm)

B 1997.7.4

30 *Campagna di Roma*, 1843

Graphite with white gouache
on gray wove paper
3 ¼ x 6 ¾ in. (8.3 x 17.1 cm)

Inscribed lower left: *Campagna di Roma*;
lower right: *E. Lear. del. 1843*

B 1997.7.46

29

30

31

32

31 *Leonessa*, 3 October 1844

Pen and brown ink and watercolor over pencil on beige wove paper
12 ⅛ x 10 ⅜ in. (30.8 x 26.4 cm)

Inscribed lower left: *Leonessa Santa Maria fuori della Porta / Oct. 3. 1844*; with other notations

B 1997.7.48

32 *Illustrated Excursions in Italy*
London: Thomas McLean, 1846

Shown: Plate 9, *Solomona*
Lithograph

Paul Mellon Collection

Lear's second travel book was considerably more ambitious than *Views in Rome and Its Environs*. It appeared in two volumes (the first is exhibited), with a total of fifty-five lithographs and fifty-three wood-engraved vignettes. The first volume is based on excursions Lear made in the Abruzzi in 1842. Lear drew the text from journals he kept while traveling, augmented with historical and geographical information gleaned from earlier publications on the region. For the second volume, which covered the states of the Church, Lear confined the text to short commentaries on the illustrations. After subscribing to *Views in Rome and its Environs* and the first volume of *Illustrated Excursions in Italy*, Queen Victoria requested a series of twelve drawing lessons from Lear in the summer of 1846.

33 *View near Palermo*, 1847
SEE PAGE 17

Pen and brown ink with watercolor
over graphite
12 ½ x 19 ⅛ in. (31.8 x 48.6 cm)

Inscribed center left: *May 8. 1847 / No. 1*

Paul Mellon Collection
B1975.3.968

Lear had visited Sicily in the spring of 1842.
In the late spring and early summer of 1847,
he returned. Of his earlier visit to Palermo,
he had written: "Palermo I think pleased me
more than any city I ever was in—& we saw
enough of it to know it—being there for 3
weeks owing to the illness of one of our party.
In a beautiful little plain quite walled in with
mountains—and close on the edge of the
sea—with two hills like wings forming its
harbour—Palermo is as it were shut out
from the rest of the world, & is a sort of
Naples as to situation, but without the nasty
vulgar noisy feeling that odious town always
gives me."[1]

1   Letter to the 13th Earl of Derby, June 5, 1842, *Selected
    Letters*, p. 55.

34

34 *Reggio*, 26 July 1847

Pen and brown ink over graphite on heavy
beige wove paper
11 ¼ x 18 ⅞ in. (28.6 x 47.9 cm)

Inscribed lower left: *Reggio / 26. July. 1847*;
with other notations

B1997.7.50

35

35 *Santa Decca, Corfu*, 28 May 1848 (126)

Brown ink over graphite
12 x 19 ⅞ in. (30.5 x 50.5 cm)

Inscribed lower left: *S. Decca / 28. May.
1848*; lower right: *124*; with other notations

B 1997.7.351

Lear first visited Corfu in 1848 on the invitation of George Bowen, rector of the university
there. Corfu and the other Ionian Islands had
been under British control since 1815. When
his friend Franklin Lushington was appointed
judge to the Supreme Court of Justice in the
Ionian Islands in 1855, Lear returned to the
island and made it his base of operations in
the Mediterranean until the British trans-
ferred the Ionian Islands to Greece in 1863.
The view from Santa Decca, some six or
seven miles from the city of Corfu, looking
down through olive groves to the Citadel and
across the Channel to the Albanian mountains, was one to which Lear returned again
and again (see cat. 56).

Suez, 1849

1 Letter to Fortescue, February 12, 1848,
   Selected Letters, p. 65.

2 Letter to the 13th Earl of Derby, January 12, 1849,
   Selected Letters, p. 97.

3 Letter to Ann Lear, January 17, 1849,
   Selected Letters, p. 99.

From early in 1848, Lear was thinking about a trip to Egypt. He wrote to his friend Chichester Fortescue: "The contemplation of Egypt must fill the mind—the Artistic mind I mean—with great food for the rumination of long years."[1] After nine months of traveling through the eastern Mediterranean, Lear finally reached Egypt in January 1849. The visit, however, was brief. In Cairo he met up with his friend John Cross, with whom he set out for Sinai and Palestine, but Lear gave up the trip. He would return to Egypt in 1853 and finally visit Palestine in 1858.

Lear found Cairo "so remarkable that I cannot describe it," instead recommending to his correspondent the works of Edward Lane, which "give a better account of it than I can."[2] Suez, on the other hand, was "a most stupid place, without any interest at all." What did interest Lear were the camels. A letter to his sister Ann, written the day before he drew the sheet of studies (cat. 38) contains a lengthy discussion of the animals, including this comment: "As for the camels themselves—I cannot say much for them;—they are quite harmless & quiet, but seem the most odious beasts—except when they are moving. The sort of horrible way in which they growl & snarl if you go 6 feet near them—is quite frightful—& if you did not know them—you would suppose they were going to eat you. They do the same to their own masters the Arabs—& appear to have the most unsociable disposition in the world—even among themselves."[3]

36 *Near Suez*, evening, 15 January 1849 (43)

Pen and brown ink with watercolor over graphite

5 ¼ x 9 ⅛ in. (13.3 x 23.2 cm)

Inscribed lower left: *Near Suez / evening Jany 15 1849*; lower right: *43*

B 1997.7.52

38

37 *Near Suez,* 1 pm, 16 January 1849 (48)
SEE PAGE 18

Pen and brown ink with watercolor
over graphite
5 ¼ x 9 in. (13.3 x 22.9 cm)

Inscribed lower left: *January 16. 1849 / 1 P.M. /
near Suez;* center right: *48*

B 1997.7.53

38 *Outside the Walls of Suez,* 8:30 am,
17 January 1849 (54)

Pen and brown ink with watercolor
over graphite
7 ⅝ x 5 ⅛ in. (19.4 x 13 cm)

Inscribed lower left: *outside walls of Suez /
8 ½ AM / Jany 17 / 1849;*
center right: *outside the walls of Suez;*
lower right: *54;* with other notations

B 1997.7.54

39 *Journals of a Landscape Painter
in Albania, &c.*
London: Richard Bentley, 1851

Shown: Plate 5, *Tyrana*

Paul Mellon Collection

In this volume Lear returned to the combination of lithographic illustrations and text
drawn from his own journals that he had
used in the first volume of his *Illustrated
Excursions in Italy*. The format, however, was
smaller, and the balance between illustrations
and text was more heavily weighted in favor
of the text. This format was followed in
Lear's *Journals of a Landscape Painter in
Southern Calabria, &c.* published the following year (cat. 40), and he seems to have considered it the model for a whole series of
published journals on his various travels
around the Mediterranean. When in 1863 he
published the larger format *Views in the
Seven Ionian Islands* with only short descriptive texts (cat. 59), he hoped that it would
"hold up or pave a way to my more general
smaller sized Topography of Greece, to be
one day printed with my Journals."[1] The
hoped for volume never appeared.

*Journals of a Landscape Painter in Albania,
&c* records Lear's travels through Albania and
northern Greece in the autumn of 1848 and
again in the spring of 1849. While Lear was
not the first western European to visit
Albania — Lord Byron was a particularly
prominent predecessor — and Lear scrupu-
lously recorded the authors of earlier English
works on Albania, he also claimed that his
accounts of certain parts of Albania were the
first to be published in the west.

39

40

Lear found Tyrana "wretched and disgusting" but redeemed in part by its "religious architecture and spacious market places." (p. 101). Later in the text he noted: "In no part of Albania are there such beautiful mosques." (p. 106).

1 Letter to Fortescue, August 9, 1863, *Letters*, p. 284.

40 *Journals of a Landscape Painter in Southern Calabria, &c.*
London: Richard Bentley, 1852

Shown: Plate 10, *Pass of Cánalo*
Lithograph

Paul Mellon Collection

Lear based this volume on journals written during tours of the south of Italy made in the autumn of 1847. In the preface he notes works on the region by Henry Swinburne, R. Keppel Craven, and Arthur Strutt but defends the value of his own treatment on the grounds that he is providing a "Landscape-painter's Guide-Book." (p vi).

Lear visited Cánalo after its being described to him as "un luogo tutto orrido, ed al modo vostro pittoresco" ("a place altogether horrible; and, after your fashion, picturesque"). While the natives were clearly bemused by the foreigner's taste for such forbidding terrain, Lear fully relished its sublimity: "We gradually rose into a world of stern rocks — a wilderness of terror, such as it is not easy to describe or imagine." (pp. 134-135).

Greece and Albania, 1856-1857

After Lear established himself in Corfu in 1855, he made visits to Albania in the spring of 1856 and again in the spring of 1857 (cat. 43-47) and traveled in Greece from August to October 1856.

41 *Greek Woodcutter*, 13 June 1856 (3)

Pen and brown ink with watercolor over graphite

9 ¹⁄₁₆ x 6 ⅛ in. (23 x 15.6 cm)

Inscribed lower left: *3*;
lower right: *June 13 / 56* Καροπισκόπος
[Karopiskópos] */ 3*

B 1997.7.57

42 *Corfu from Ascension*, c. 1856-64

Oil on canvas

13 ½ x 21 ½ in. (27.9 x 54.2 cm)

Signed lower left with EL monogram

Gift of Mr. and Mrs. Michael Coe

B 1979.11

41

42

43 *Vjöse*, 12:30 pm, 16 April 1857

Pen and brown ink with watercolor
over graphite

4 ⅞ x 7 ⅝ in. (12.4 x 19.4 cm)

Inscribed lower left: *Viosa / 16 April (12.30) /
1857*; with other notations

B 1997.7.59

44 *Vjöse*, 7:15 pm 17 April 1857

Pen and brown ink with watercolor
over graphite

5 ¹⁄₁₆ x 7 ⁹⁄₁₆ in. (12.4 x 19.2 cm)

Inscribed lower left: Κλεισόρα [Klisora]
17 April 1857. 7.15 P.M.

B 1997.7.60

43

44

45

45 *Tepelene*, 18 April 1857

Pen and brown ink with watercolor
over graphite

5 ⅛ x 7 ⅝ in. (13 x 19.4 cm)

Inscribed lower left: *Tepelene / 18. April 1857*;
with other notations

B 1997.7.62

46 *Tepelene*, 19 April 1857

Pen and brown ink with watercolor
over graphite

5 ⅛ x 7 ⅝ in. (13 x 19.4 cm)

Inscribed lower right: Δεροπούλι
[Derópouli] / *Tepelene / 19. April. / 1857*;
with other notations

B 1997.7.63

46

47 *On the Road, Two Hours from Tepelene,*
    19 April 1857

Pen and brown ink with watercolor
over graphite
9 9/16 x 13 1/8 in. (24.3 x 33.3 cm)

Inscribed lower left: *19. April / 1857 /
2 hours from Tepelene*; lower right:
on the road, 2 hours from Τεπεδελένη
[Tepelene];
with other notations

B 1997.7.64

47

48

48 *Mount Athos and the Monastery of Stavroniketes*, 1857

Oil on canvas
13 ½ x 21 ½ in. (34.3 x 54.6 cm)

Paul Mellon Collection

B 1981.25.151

Back in Corfu after a two month tour of Greece, with three weeks spent on Mount Athos, Lear wrote to Fortescue of "THE Holy Mountain, altogether the most surprising thing I have seen in my travels, perhaps baring Egypt." He related: "It is a peninsular mountain about 2000 ft. high & 50 miles long ending in a vast crag, near 7000 feet high, this being Athos. All but this bare crag is one mass of vast forest, beech, chestnut, oak, & ilex, and all round the cliffs and crags by the sea are 20 great and ancient monistirries, not to speak of 6 or 700 little 'uns above and below and around. These convents are inhabited by, altogether perhaps, 6 or 7000 monx, & as you may have heard, no female creature exists in all the peninsula:—there are nothing but mules, tomcats, & cocks allowed. This is literally true."

Lear and his servant Giorgio both fell ill with fever in Athos; according to Lear, Giorgio almost died. "However I persisted & persisted & finally I got drawings of every one of the 20 big monasteries, so that such a valuable collection is hardly to be found." Lear was both fascinated and appalled by Athos: "However wondrous and picturesque the exterior & interior of the monasteries, & however abundantly & exquisitely glorious & stupendous the scenery of the mountain, I would not go again... so gloomy, so shockingly unnatural, so lonely, so lying, so unatonably odious seems to me all the atmosphere of such monkery."[1]

1 Letter to Fortescue, October 9, 1856, *Letters*, pp. 40-41.

49 *St. Kiven and the Gentle Kathleen*
SEE PAGE 10

8 original manuscript pages
Pen and brown ink on laid paper

Lear's earliest efforts at nonsense were paro-
dies of well-known authors and humorous
illustrations to the verse of others, such as the
popular Irish poet Thomas Moore. *St. Kiven
and the Gentle Kathleen* is adapted from a
poem by Moore.

50 *A Book of Nonsense*
London: Thomas McLean, 1846

Shown: *There was an Old Man of Corfu…*

Paul Mellon Collection

Lear published his first book of nonsense
verse and drawings in 1846, not under his
own name but as "Derry down Derry."
Most of the thirty-six limericks in the volume
had been composed at Knowsley in the 1830s
for the entertainment of the children in
the house. When a third, much expanded,
edition was published in 1861, it bore Lear's
name on the title page. That edition enjoyed
great popular success, and Lear's reputation
as a humorist began to eclipse his reputation
as a topographical artist.

THERE WAS AN OLD MAN OF CORFU, WHO NEVER KNEW WHAT HE SHOULD DO;
SO HE RUSHED UP AND DOWN, TILL THE SUN MADE HIM BROWN,
THAT BEWILDERED OLD MAN OF CORFU.

50

C. was a Camel, —
They rode on his hump,
— But if you fell off,
you came down such a bump!
C !
O what a high Camel !

51

51 *Alphabet*, 1857

Original manuscript
Pen and brown ink on 26 sheets
mounted on linen

Inscribed at the end of the volume:
*Alphabet, written & illustrated by
Edward Lear / 1857 / for Winifred[,] William
& Barrington Crake. / The book was made by
their aunt Mary Ann Crake.*

Paul Mellon Collection

One of a number of manuscript alphabets
Lear produced for the children of his
acquaintance, this was produced for the
children of Vandeleur Benjamin Crake, a
Sussex county magistrate.

52 *The Dead Sea*, 16 and 17 April 1858 (60)

Pen and brown ink with watercolor
over graphite
14 ½ x 21 ¾ in. (36.8 x 55.2 cm)

Inscribed lower right: *16 & 17 April 1858
(60)*; with other notations

Paul Mellon Collection
B 1975.4.1933

Lear visited Palestine in the spring of 1858,
arriving in Jerusalem during Holy Week.
Finding the city crowded and unpleasant, he
quickly set off for Petra, Masada, and the
Dead Sea, which he described tersely as
"a wonder in its way."[1] This sketch records
the view looking southeast across the
southern end of the Dead Sea, with the salt
mountain of Usdum (Sodom) rising at the
far right. Among his inscriptions are several
attempts to identify the location in this
region still rarely visited by westerners.
"Wady Mabookos?" is perhaps Lear's own
tentative attempt at a place name. "Wady
Mubughgik (Lynch)" and "Wady Maiet-
Embarrheg / de Saulcy?" show Lear trying to
relate his position to the two accounts that
served as his authorities on the geography of
the area: William Francis Lynch's *Narrative
of the United States' Expedition to the River
Jordan and the Dead Sea*, 1849, and Louis
Félicien Joseph Caignart de Saulcy's *Narrative
of a Journey round the Dead Sea, and in the
Bible Lands,* 1853.

1 Letter to Lady Waldegrave, May 27, 1858, *Letters*,
p. 108.

52

53

53 *Jericho*, 7 May 1858 (157)

Pen and brown ink with watercolor
over graphite
7 ⅛ x 19 ⅞ in. (18.1 x 50.5 cm)

Inscribed lower right: *Jericho / May 7. 1858 /
(157)*; with other notations

Paul Mellon Collection
B 1975.4.1932

After visiting the Dead Sea and Jericho, Lear
returned to Jerusalem and then traveled on to
Lebanon. By late summer he was back in
London, where in the autumn the sculptor
Thomas Woolner met Lear at the home of
Holman Hunt. Lear showed his Palestinian
sketches, which Woolner declared "the most
beautiful things he has ever done," interesting
"not only for the mystery and history
attached to the places themselves but also for
the excessive fineness, tenderness and beauty
of the art displayed in them."[1]

1 Woolner, letter to Emily Tennyson, October 22, 1858,
   quoted in Noakes 1985, p. 112.

54 *Zagóri, Greece*, 1860
SEE PAGE 8

Oil on canvas
15 ½ x 10 in. (39.4 x 25.4 cm)

Signed lower left with
EL monogram and dated: *1860*

B1997.7.7

55 *Butrinto, Albania*, 1861

Oil on canvas
13 ½ x 21 ½ in. (34.3 x 54.6 cm)

Signed lower right with EL monogram

B 1997.7.6

56 *Corfu from Santa Decca*, 1862
SEE PAGE 19

Oil on canvas
13 ½ x 21 ½ in. (34.3 x 54.6 cm)

Signed lower right with EL monogram

B 1997.7.1

57 *Philae, Egypt*, 1863

Oil on canvas
10 ¹³⁄₁₆ x 21 ½ in. (34.3 x 54.6 cm)

Signed in pen and black ink on the original
stretcher and dated: *June 15, 1863.*
Inscribed on the stretcher?: *Philae / Painted
by me in 1863 for Mrs. William Rawson from
drawings made at Philae in 1854.*

Paul Mellon Collection
B 1974.3.12

55

57

58

58 *Orange Trees*, 3 April 1863

Pen and brown ink with watercolor
over graphite
10 x 16 ¹³⁄₁₆ in. (25.4 x 42.7cm)

Inscribed lower left: Αγριοκήπιον
Βασιλάκης [Vasilakis Orchard] /
3 April. 1863; verso: 18 / upright / Lowest

Gift of Chauncey Brewster Tinker
B1975.6.102

59 *Views in the Seven Ionian Islands*
London: Edward Lear, 1863

Shown: *Capo Ducato, or Sappho's Leap, Santa Maura*
Colored lithograph

Beinecke Rare Book and Manuscript Library

Knowing that, with the ceding of the Ionian Islands to Greece, his time there was coming to an end, Lear made a tour of the islands from March to June of 1863. The result of the tour was another volume of lithographic views, which Lear hoped would have the attraction of topicality. As he wrote in the introduction: "At a time when so great a change in the destiny of these Islands is about to occur, the present book, illustrative of places, hereafter perhaps, to be as little visited by our countrymen as they have been familiarly known to them for nearly half a century, may have a more than ordinary claim to be thought interesting." He confided to Fortescue that this was not the serious work on Greece that he wanted to publish but that its hoped-for success might make possible that other work: "My plan was to bring out a work consisting of 20 Ionian views… This collection would, you see, have given the beastly public all that was most characteristic of the Islands: and, being well done, if at all, would keep up my prestige as a draftsman of Mediterranean scenery — and would, moreover, hold up or pave a way to my more general smallersized Topography of Greece, to be one day printed with my Journals."[1]

Capo Ducato is the southwestern point of the island of Santa Maura, the ancient Leucas. Byron's Childe Harold "saw the evening star above Leucadia's far-projecting rock of woe." In antiquity, Sappho supposedly leapt to her death from the cliff.

59

1 Letter to Fortescue, August 9, 1863, *Letters*, p. 284.

The Nile Tour, 1867

In December 1866 Lear wrote to Lady Waldegrave that he had made up his mind "to go for a Nile and Palestine move." His intention was to travel along the upper Nile, which he had never reached in his earlier visits: "My objects on the Nile are, (excepting only to draw Denderah on the lower river,) wholly above Philae—as I never saw Nubia, and particularly wish to get drawings of Ipsambûl, and Ibreêm."[1] He was not disappointed, writing to Lady Waldegrave again in March: "Nubia delighted me; it isn't a bit like Egypt, except that theres a river in both. Sad, stern, uncompromising landscape—dark ashy purple lines of hills—piles of granite rocks—fringes of palm—& ever and anon astonishing ruins of oldest Temples:—above all wonderful—Aboo Simbel which took my breath away. The 2d. Cataract also is very interesting—& at Philae & Denderah I got new subjects—beside scores & scores of little atomy illustrations all the way up & down the river."[2]

Lear hoped to publish the Nile tour as one of the series of his "Journals of a Landscape Painter." The following year he wrote from Cannes: "At present I am not drawing at all nor painting—but writing: the rough copy of my Cretan journals is done, and nearly that of the Nile 1854: the Nubia of 1867 will follow, and I mean to get all three ready for publication with illustrations, if possible next summer, whether in parts or volumes I can't yet say."[3] None of the three projected volumes was published.

1 Letter to Lady Waldegrave, December 11, 1866, *Later Letters*, p. 80.
2 Letter to Lady Waldegrave, March 9, 1867, *Selected Letters*, pp. 208-209.
3 Letter to Lady Waldegrave, January 9, 1868, *Later Letters*, p. 91.

60 *Sowadi*, 8:30 am, 4 January 1867 (65)

Pen and brown ink with watercolor
over graphite
5 ½ x 9 ³⁄₁₆ in. (14 x 23.3 cm)

Inscribed lower left: *Sowadi. 8.30. Jany. 4.
1867*; lower right: *(65)*; with other notations

B 1997.7.86

61 *Kom el Amhr*, 1:00 pm, 4 January 1867 (68)

Pen and brown ink with watercolor
over graphite
5 ½ x 9 ³⁄₁₆ in. (14 x 23.3 cm)

Inscribed lower left: *Kom el Amhr. 1. PM.
Jany 4. 1867*; lower right: *(68)*;
with other notations

B 1997.7.87

62 *Opposite Melaghara*, 5:20 pm,
4 January 1867 (71)

Pen and brown ink with watercolor
over graphite
2 ³⁄₈ x 5 ⅞ in. (6 x 14.9 cm)

Inscribed lower left: *opposite Melaghara
5.20 PM*; lower right: *71*; with other notations

B 1997.7.89

60

61

62

63

64

63 *Sheikh Abadeh*, 3:15 pm, 6 January 1867 (84)

Pen and brown ink with watercolor
over graphite
2 ⅝ x 10 in. (6.7 x 25.4 cm)

Inscribed lower left: *Sheikh Abadeh. 3.15 PM.
Jany 6. 1867*; lower right: *(84)*;
with other notations

B 1997.7.93

64 *Sheikh Abadeh*, 3:20 pm, 6 January 1867 (85)

Pen and brown ink with watercolor
over graphite
2 ⅜ x 10 in. (6 x 25.4 cm)

Inscribed lower left: *3.20 PM Jany 6. 1867.
Sheikh Abadeh*; lower right: *(85)*;
with other notations

B 1997.7.94

"Shekh Abadeh seemed extremely beautiful —
for luxuriousness of palms, & 2 mosque towers:
but I could not even see the columns which
were there in 1853. O, City of the days of
Adrian! I can't describe what it is, but there is
a great charm about this same Antinöopolis.
—The walk to Melaus was more interesting
agriculturally than otherwise: such tracts of
sugar cane! And a steam working engine,
which grunts & whistles as it might do at
Kings Cross. The Copt parties returning
home are most picturesque & indeed every
moment of Nile life has its pictures:
camels — buffalos — donkeys — costumes —
pigeon houses &c. &c."[1]

1 Diary, January 6, 1867, manuscript, Houghton
Library, Harvard University.

65 *Abydos*, 1:00 pm, 12 January 1867 (134)

Pen and gray ink with watercolor
over graphite
6 ⅛ x 12 in. (15.6 x 30.5 cm)

Inscribed lower left: *Abydus. 1. PM.
January 12. 1867*; lower right: *(134)*;
with other notations

B 1997.7.120

According to the Egyptologist John Gardner
Wilkinson, who provided the text for
Murray's *Handbook for Travellers in Egypt*,
the "grand scale" and "considerable antiquity"
of the ruins "evince the importance of
Abydus, and show that it yielded to few cities
of Upper Egypt in size and magnificence."[1]
Considered the burial place of Osiris, Abydos
was a desired place of interment for the rich
and powerful throughout ancient Egypt.

1 John Gardner Wilkinson, *Handbook for Travellers
   in Egypt*, 2nd edition (London: John Murray, 1858),
   p. 312.

66 *Dendera*, 15 January 1867 (155)

Pen and brown ink with watercolor
over graphite
3 ⅛ x 10 1/16 in. (7.9 x 25.6 cm)

Inscribed lower left: *Denderah Jany 15. 1867*;
lower right: *(155)*; with other notations

B 1997.7.126

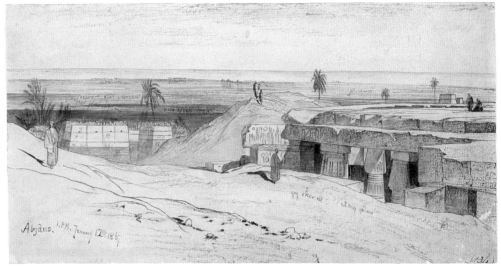

65

66

67

68

69

67 *Dendera*, 9:00 am, 15 January 1867 (156)

Pen and brown ink with watercolor and gouache over graphite on beige wove paper
3 ⅜ x 10 ½ in. (8.6 x 26.7 cm)

Inscribed lower left: *Dendera. / 9. AM. 15. Jany 1867*; lower right: *(156)*; with other notations

B 1997.7.127

68 *Dendera*, 9:15 am, 15 January 1867 (157)

Pen and brown ink with watercolor and gouache over graphite on beige wove paper
3 ¼ x 10 ½ in. (8.3 x 26.7 cm)

Inscribed lower left: *Denderah / 9.15 AM / 15 Jany 1867*; lower right: *(157)*; with other notations

B 1997.7.128

69 *Dendera*, 15 January 1867 (158)

Pen and brown ink with watercolor and gouache over graphite on beige wove paper
2 ⅞ x 12 ⅝ in. (7.3 x 32.1 cm)

Inscribed lower left: *Déndera. 15 Jany 1867*; lower right: *(158)*; with other notations

B 1997.7.129

The temple at Dendera, dedicated to the goddess Hathor, is an example of late Egyptian architecture. In Murray's *Handbook*, Wilkinson offered the opinion: "From its superior state of preservation it deserves a distinguished rank among the most interesting monuments of Egypt."[1]

1 Wilkinson, p. 316.

70 *Near Negadeh*, 12:30 pm,
17 January 1867 (188)

Pen and gray ink with watercolor
over graphite
2 ⅝ x 9 ¾ in. (6.7 x 24.8 cm)

Inscribed lower left: *12.30. pm. 17 Jany. 1867
east side near Nagadeh*; lower right: *(188)*;
with other notations

B 1997.7.137

70

71 *Negadeh*, 1:45 pm, 17 January 1867 (190)

Pen and gray ink with watercolor
over graphite
3 ¹¹⁄₁₆ x 9 ⁷⁄₁₆ in. (9.4 x 24 cm)

Inscribed lower left: *1.45 pm. Nagádeh.
17. Jany. 1867*; lower right: *(190)*;
with other notations

B 1997.7.138

Negadeh was noted for its Coptic and
Catholic convents. In his diary, Lear noted:
"Pass Nagadeh at 1:30. What a place of
pigeons! There is a new white church since I
was here in 1854. The place has a curious
look."[1]

1 Diary, January 17, 1867, Manuscript, Houghton
Library, Harvard University.

71

72

73

72 *Luxor*, 7:00 am, 20 January 1867 (198)

Pen and brown ink with watercolor and gouache over graphite on gray wove paper
3 9/16 x 10 3/8 in. (9 x 26.4 cm)

Inscribed lower left: *El Uksor. 7. am. 20 Jany 1867*; lower right: *(198)*; with other notations

B 1997.7.140

73 *Luxor*, 7:30 am, 20 January 1867 (199)

Pen and brown ink with watercolor and gouache over graphite on gray wove paper
3 1/8 x 10 3/8 in. (7.9 x 26.4 cm)

Inscribed lower left: *El Luxor 7.30. am. 20 Jany 1867*; lower right: *(199)*; with other notations

B 1997.7.141

74 *Karnak*, 9:30 pm, 22 January 1867 (212)

Pen and black ink with watercolor
over graphite
3 ½ x 6 ¾ in.

Inscribed lower left: *9.30 PM*; lower right:
Karnak 22 Jany 1867 212

B 1997.7.145

75 *Karnak*, 10:00 pm, 22 January 1867 (213)

Pen and black ink with watercolor
over graphite
3 ⁵⁄₁₆ x 6 ¾ in. (8.4 x 17.1 cm)

Inscribed lower left: *Karnak / 22 Jany 1867
10 PM*; lower right: *213*

B 1997.7.146

The celebrated temple complexes of Luxor
and Karnak lie on the east bank of the Nile
at the site of Thebes, for centuries the capital
of ancient Egypt. In the exhibition are views of
the Great Temple of Amon at Karnak by
William James Müller (cat. 187) and David
Roberts (cat. 193). In marked contrast to
Müller and Roberts, who situate the viewer
within the colossal remains of the temple, Lear
concentrates on the surrounding landscape.

74

75

76

76 *Shelaal*, 2:30 am, 29 January 1867 (260)

Pen and black ink with watercolor and gouache over graphite on beige wove paper
2 ⅞ x 10 ¾ in. (7.3 x 27.3 cm)

Inscribed lower left: *Shelaal. 2.30. PM. Jany 29 1867*; lower right: *(260)*; with other notations

B 1997.7.163

77

77 *Shelaal*, 5:30 am, 29 January 1867 (264)

Pen and black ink with watercolor and gouache over graphite on beige wove paper
2 ¹⁵⁄₁₆ x 10 ¹¹⁄₁₆ in. (7.5 x 27.1 cm)

Inscribed lower left: *Shelaal 5.30. PM. 29. Jany. 1867*; lower right: *(264)*; with other notations

B 1997.7.164

78 *Philae*, 5:20 pm, 30 January 1867 (275)

Pen and brown ink with watercolor
over graphite
3 9/16 x 7 3/16 in. (9 x 18.3 cm)

Inscribed lower left: *Philae / 30 Jany 1867. /
5.20 PM*; lower right: *275*;
with other notations

B 1997.7.167

79 *Philae*, 6:00-6:15 am, 31 January 1867 (277)

Pen and brown ink with watercolor over
graphite on gray wove paper
2 1/8 x 5 3/8 in. (5.4 x 13.7 cm)

Inscribed lower left: *6-6.15 AM.
31 Jany 1867*; lower right: *(277)*;
with other notations

B 1997.7.168

The temple island of Philae was a favorite
site of Lear, who had spent ten days there
during his Egyptian tour of 1854. He produced at least twenty oil paintings of Philae,
one of which is included in the exhibition
(cat. 57).

80 *Dehmyt*, 7:30 am, 31 January 1867 (278)

Pen and brown ink with watercolor over
graphite on gray wove paper
2 7/8 x 10 5/8 in. (7.3 x 27 cm)

Inscribed lower left: *7.30 AM 31 Jany.1867.
Dehmyt*; lower right: *(278)*;
with other notations

B 1997.7.169

78

79

80

81

82

81 *Gertassee*, 9:10 am, 31 January 1867 (284)

Pen and brown ink with watercolor
over graphite
2 ⁷⁄₁₆ x 6 ¹⁵⁄₁₆ in. (6.2 x 17.6 cm)

Inscribed lower left: *9.10. AM. 31 Jany 1867*
(temple light off sky) Gertasse;
lower right: *(284)*; with other notations

B 1997.7.171

"Nearly 9—Gertasse—which is most beautiful—perched on high slopes of sand rock,
& as there is now but little wind—I draw it.
But at 9:30, wind increases & the small sail is
taken down."[1]

1 Diary, January 31, 1867, Manuscript, Houghton
Library, Harvard University.

82 *Near Tafa*, 9:45 am, 31 January 1867 (287)

Pen and brown ink with watercolor and
gouache over graphite on gray wove paper
2 ⅝ x 10 ⅝ in. (6.7 x 27 cm)

Inscribed lower left: *9.45. AM. 31 Jany 1867.*
near Tápha; lower right: *287*;
with other notations

B 1997.7.172

83 *Tafa*, 10:15 am, 31 January 1867 (289)

Pen and brown ink with watercolor
over graphite
2 ⅜ x 6 ¹⁵⁄₁₆ in. (6 x 17.6 cm)

Inscribed lower left: *Táfa 10.15. AM
31 Jany 1867*; lower right *(289)*;
with other notations

B 1997.7.173

"Towards 10—near Tafa. 2 temples—both
pretty. I had no idea of the beauty of Nubia
scenery before coming here."[1]

1 Diary, January 31, 1867, Manuscript, Houghton
Library, Harvard University.

84 *Dendour*, 2:15 pm, 31 January 1867 (298)
SEE PAGE 38

Pen and brown ink with watercolor and
gouache over graphite on gray wove paper
2 ¾ x 7 in. (7 x 17.8 cm)

Inscribed lower left: *Dendour 2.15. PM.
31. Jany 1867*; lower right: *(298)*;
with other notations

B1997.7.174

85 *Near Garf Hossayn*, 3:40 pm,
31 January 1867 (299)
SEE PAGE 39

Pen and brown ink with watercolor
over graphite
2 ⁵⁄₁₆ x 6 ¹⁵⁄₁₆ in. (5.9 x 17.6 cm)

Inscribed lower left: *near Garf Hosayn /
3.40 PM. Jany. 31. 1867*; lower right: *(299)*;
with other notations

B 1997.7.175

83

87

88

89

90

86 *Near Mereeh or Garf Hossayn*, 4:00 pm,
31 January 1867 (302)
SEE PAGE 40

Pen and brown ink with watercolor and
gouache over graphite on gray wove paper
2 5/16 x 7 in. (5.9 x 17.8 cm)

Inscribed lower left: *near Merieh or
Garf Hosayn. 4. PM. 31. Jany. 1867*;
lower right: *302*; with other notations

B 1997.7.176

87 *Ibreem*, 10:00 am, 2 February 1867 (317)

Pen and brown ink with watercolor over graphite
2 7/16 x 6 7/8 in. (6.2 x 17.5 cm)

Inscribed lower left: *10. AM. 2. Feby. 1867.
Ibreem*; lower right: *317*; with other notations

B 1997.7.183

88 *Ibreem*, 10:30 am, 2 February 1867 (318)

Pen and brown ink with watercolor over graphite
1 11/16 x 4 7/8 in. (4.3 x 12.4 cm)

Inscribed lower left: *Ibreem. 10.30 AM. Feby 2.
1867*; lower right: *318*; with other notations

B 1997.7.184

89 *Ibreem*, 11:00 am, 2 February 1867 (319)

Pen and brown ink with watercolor over graphite
3 3/8 x 9 7/8 in. (8.6 x 25.1 cm)

Inscribed lower left: *11. AM Feby 2. 1867.
Ibreem*; lower right: *(319)*; with other notations

B 1997.7.185

90 *Between Ibreem and Wady Halfeh*,
2:45 pm, 2 February 1867 (328)

Pen and brown ink with watercolor and
gouache over graphite on beige wove paper
3 x 5 3/8 in. (7.6 x 13.7 cm)

Inscribed lower left: *2.45 PM. Feby 2. 1867*;
lower right: *328*; with other notations

B 1997.7.187

91 *Between Ibreem and Wady Halfeh*,
3:15 pm, 2 February 1867 (330)

Pen and brown ink with watercolor
over graphite
3 ½ x 6 in. (8.9 x 15.2 cm)

Inscribed lower left: *3.15 PM Feby 2. 1867*;
lower right: *(330)*

B 1997.7.188

Lear reached Wady Halfeh, just below the
Second Cataract, on February 3. This would
be the uppermost point of Lear's tour.

92 *Abu Simbel*, 9:00 am, 8 February 1867 (372A)

Pen and brown ink with watercolor
over graphite
5 ¹⁄₁₆ x 7 ½ in. (12.9 x 19.1 cm)

Inscribed lower left: *Aboo Simbl. 9. AM.
8 Feby 1867*; lower right: *(372)/A*

B 1997.7.205

The temples at Abu Simbel were carved into
the sandstone cliffs during the reign of
Rameses II. According to Wilkinson, they
constitute "the most interesting remains met
with in Nubia, and, excepting Thebes, during
the whole valley of the Nile."[1] Lear was
much affected by his encounter: "Arrived
& moored below the small temple at 9. But
in turning the corner of the rocks—forth
suddenly came the Rameses Heads!! I was
absolutely too astonished & affected to draw
—so I lost any sketch & must go back for it."[2]

1 Wilkinson, p. 425.

2 Diary, February 8, 1867, Manuscript, Houghton
Library, Harvard University.

91

92

93

94

93 *Abu Simbel*, 11-11:30 am, 8 February 1867
(374)

Pen and brown ink with watercolor
over graphite
13 ¾ x 20 ⅝ in. (34.9 x 51.1 cm)

Inscribed lower left: *Abou Simbl 11-11.30 AM. /
8 Feby. 1867*; lower right: *(374)*;
with other notations

Paul Mellon Collection

B1975.4.1559

94 *Abu Simbel*, 4:30 pm, 8 February 1867 (379)

Pen and brown ink with watercolor
over graphite
3 ⁷⁄₁₆ x 9 ⅞ in. (8.7 x 25.1 cm)

Inscribed lower left: *Abou Simbl. 4.30.
8 Feby. 1867*; lower right: *(379)*

B1997.7.206

"Abou Simbl is a most ungovernably difficult
affair to draw or make anything of—as one
is too close to the little temple, & too near &
too far above the big one. But as a whole, the
scene is overpowering for its beauty—
color—solitude—history—art—poetry—
every sort of association."[1]

1 Diary, February 8, 1867, Manuscript, Houghton
Library, Harvard University.

95   *Abu Simbel*, 10:30 am, 9 February 1867 (383)

Pen and brown ink with watercolor and
gouache over graphite on beige wove paper
3 ⅞ x 10 1/16 in. (9.8 x 25.6 cm)

Inscribed lower left: *10.30 AM Feby 9. 1867.*
Abou Simbl; lower right: *(383)*;
with other notations

B 1997.7.208

96   *Abu Simbel*, 1:00 pm, 9 February 1867 (384)

Pen and brown ink with watercolor and
gouache over graphite on beige wove paper
3 ⅞ x 10 1/16 in. (9.8 x 25.6 cm)

Inscribed lower left: *1. PM. Feby 9. 1867.*
Abou Simbl; Lower right: *(384)*;
with other notations

B 1997.7.209

97   *Abu Simbel*, 1:10 pm, 9 February 1867 (385)

Pen and brown ink with watercolor and
gouache over graphite on beige wove paper
3 ⅜ x 9 ⅞ in. (8.6 x 25.1 cm)

Inscribed lower left: *Abou Simbl 9 Feby.*
1.10 PM 1867; lower right: *(385)*;
with other notations

B 1997.7.210

"On deck till 1.30. Last memorials of Abou
Simbl—(the position of which I certainly
never saw given in any drawing—tho of
near views many,) a place earliest known to
me from the tales of my dear sister Ann—48
years ago."[1]

1 Diary, February 9, 1867, Manuscript, Houghton
Library, Harvard University.

95

96

97

98

99

98   *Ibreem*, 10:00 pm, 10 February 1867 (404)

Pen and gray ink with watercolor
over graphite
3 ⁷⁄₁₆ x 9 ⅞ in. (8.7 x 25.1 cm)

Inscribed lower left: *10. PM. Feby 10. 1867
Ibreem*; lower right: *(404)*;
with other notations

B 1997.7.214

99   *Ibreem*, 6:30 am, 11 February 1867 (405)

Pen and gray ink with watercolor
over graphite
3 ⅜ x 9 ⅞ in. (8.6 x 25.1 cm)

Inscribed lower left: *Ibreem. Feby 11. 1867.
6.30 PM*; lower right: *(405)*;
with other notations

B 1997.7.215

100 *Amada*, 6:50 am, 12 February 1867 (419)

Pen and brown ink with watercolor
over graphite
3 9/16 x 6 7/8 in. (9 x 17.5 cm)

Inscribed lower left: *Amàda. / 6.50 AM /
Feby. 12. 1867*; lower right: *(419)*;
with other notations

B 1997.7.217

101 *Amada*, 7:10 am, 12 February 1867 (420)

Pen and brown ink with watercolor
over graphite
3 9/16 x 6 7/8 in. (9 x 17.5 cm)

Inscribed lower left: *Amada / 7.10 AM
Feby. 12. 1867*; lower right: *(420)*;
with other notations

B 1997.7.218

100

101

102

102 *Amada*, 7:20 am, 12 February 1867 (421)

Pen and brown ink with watercolor
over graphite

3 ⅜ x 9 ⅞ in. (8.6 x 25.1 cm)

Inscribed lower left: *Amada. 7.20 AM
Feby.12.1867*; lower right: *(421)*;
with other notations

BI997.7.219

103

103 *Amada*, 7:25 am, 12 February 1867 (422)

Pen and brown ink with watercolor
over graphite

3 ⅝ x 6 ¹⁵⁄₁₆ in. (9.2 x 17.6 cm)

Inscribed lower left: *Amàda / 7.25. 12 Feby
1867*; lower right: *(422)*

BI997.7.220

104 *Amada*, 7:30 am, 12 February 1867 (423)

Pen and brown ink with watercolor
over graphite

2 ¼ x 10 ¼ in. (5.7 x 26 cm)

Inscribed lower left: *Amada. / 7.30. AM /
Feby 12. 1867*; lower right: *(423)*;
with other notations

BI997.7.221

104

105 *Maharraka*, 7:15 am, 14 February 1867 (462)

Pen and brown ink with watercolor
over graphite
3 ^{13}⁄₁₆ x 6 ^{13}⁄₁₆ in. (9.7 x 17.3 cm)

Inscribed lower left: *Mahárraka / 7.15 AM.
Feby 14. 1867*; lower right: *(462)*

BI997.7.229

106 *Maharraka*, 7:25 am, 14 February 1867 (463)

Pen and brown ink with watercolor
over graphite
3 ^{13}⁄₁₆ x 6 ^{13}⁄₁₆ in. (9.7 x 17.3 cm)

Inscribed lower left: *Maharraka. Feby 14.
1867 / 7.25 AM*; lower right: *(463)*

BI997.7.230

107 *Maharraka*, 7:30 am, 14 February 1867 (464)

Pen and brown ink with watercolor
over graphite
2 ½ x 6 ⅞ in. (6.3 x 17.5 cm)

Inscribed lower right: *Mahárraka / 7.30 AM /
Feby 14 1867 (464)*

B 1997.7.231

105

106

107

108

110

108 *Maharraka*, 7:35 am, 14 February 1867 (465)

Pen and brown ink with watercolor
over graphite
2 ¼ x 6 ⅞ in. (5.7 x 17.5 cm)

Inscribed lower left: *Mahárraka 7.35 AM.*
Feby 14. 1867; lower right: *(465)*;
with other notations

B1997.7.232

109 *Garf Hossayn*, 2:30 pm, 15 February 1867 (484)
SEE PAGE 28

Pen and brown ink with watercolor
over graphite
9 ½ x 13 ¾ in. (24.1 x 34.9 cm)

Inscribed lower left: *Gerf Hoseyn /*
2.30. PM. Feby. 15. 1867; lower right: *(484)*;
with other notations

B 1997.7.236

110 *Between Kalabshee and Tafa*, 5:20 pm,
16 February 1867 (502)

Pen and brown ink with watercolor
over graphite
2 x 6 ¹³⁄₁₆ in. (5.1 x 17.3 cm)

Inscribed lower left: *5.20 Feby 16. 1867.*
between Kalabshe & Tafa; lower right: *(502)*;
with other notations

B1997.7.243

111 *Near Tafa*, 5:50 pm, 16 February 1867 (505A)

Pen and brown ink with watercolor
over graphite
2 ⅜ x 6 ⅞ in. (6 x 17.5 cm)

Inscribed lower left: *5.50 pm Feby 16 1867.
near Tafa*; lower right: *A / 505*;
with other notations

BI997.7.244

112 *Near Tafa*, 6:00 pm, 16 February 1867 (507)

Pen and brown ink with watercolor
over graphite
2 ½ x 7 ⁹⁄₁₆ in. (6.3 x 19.2 cm)

Inscribed lower left: *near Tâfa. 6. PM.
Feby. 16. 1867*; lower right: *(507)*;
with other notations

BI997.7.245

113 *Near Tafa*, 6:10 pm, 16 February 1867 (508)

Pen and brown ink with watercolor
over graphite
2 ½ x 7 ½ in. (6.3 x 19.1 cm)

Inscribed lower left: *6.10 PM. Feby. 16. 1867.
Near Tafa*; lower right: *(508)*

BI997.7.246

111

112

113

114

115

114 *Karnak*, 24 February 1867 (545)

Pen and brown ink with watercolor over graphite

2 ½ x 9 ⅞ in. (6.3 x 25.1 cm)

Inscribed lower left: *Karnak / 24 Feby. 1867*; lower right: *545*

BI997.7.254

115 *Karnak*, 9:30 am, 24 February 1867 (546)

Pen and brown ink with watercolor over graphite

6 ¹¹⁄₁₆ x 9 ⅞ in. (17 x 25.1 cm)

Inscribed lower left: *Karnak. 9.30 AM. 24 Feby 1867*; lower right: *(546)*; with other notations

BI997.7.255

116 *Gebel Sheikh Abu Fodde*, 8:00 am,
4 March 1867 (588)

Pen and brown ink with watercolor
over graphite
3 ⅜ x 6 ¼ in. (8.6 x 15.9 cm)

Inscribed lower left: *G. Sheikh Abou Fodde.
March 4 - 8.* AM *1867*; lower right: *(588)*;
with other notations

BI997.7.280

116

117 *Gebel Sheikh Abu Fodde*, 7:30 am,
4 March 1867 (590)

Pen and brown ink with watercolor
over graphite
3 ⅜ x 9 ⅞ in. (8.6 x 25.1 cm)

Inscribed lower left: *Gebel Sheikh Abou
Fodde. 7.30.* AM. *March 4. 1867*;
lower right: *(590)*; with other notations

BI997.7.281

117

118 *Gebel Sheikh Abu Fodde*, 12:30 pm,
4 March 1867 (592)

Pen and brown ink with watercolor
over graphite
3 ⅝ x 9 ⅞ in. (9.2 x 25.1 cm)

Inscribed lower left: *12.30.* PM. *March 4.
1867. Gebel S. Aboufodde*; lower right: *(592)*;
with other notations

BI997.7.282

118

119

120

121

119   *Abu Fodde*, 4:00 pm, 4 March 1867 (594)

Pen and brown ink with watercolor
over graphite
3 ⅜ x 6 ¾ in. (8.6 x 17.1 cm)

Inscribed lower left: *Abou Fodde. 4. PM.
March 4. 1867*; lower right: *(594)*;
with other notations

B1997.7.283

120   *Gantara (Suez Canal)*, 5:25 am,
27 March 1867 (20)

Pen and brown ink with watercolor
over graphite
3 ⁷⁄₁₆ x 9 in. (8.7 x 22.9 cm)

Inscribed lower left: *Gántara. (Suez Canal.)
5.25. AM. March 27. 1867*; lower right: *(20)*;
with other notations

B1997.7.319

121   *Near Beer El Abt*, 4:30 pm,
28 March 1867 (23)

Pen and brown ink with watercolor
over graphite
3 ⁵⁄₁₆ x 9 ¹³⁄₁₆ in. (8.4 x 24.9 cm)

Inscribed lower left: *near (?) Beer El Abt.
4.30. PM. / March 28. 1867*;
lower right: *(23)*; with other notations

B1997.7.320

122 *Near El Areesh*, 3:30 pm, 30 March 1867 (27)

Pen and brown ink with watercolor
over graphite

4 ¹³⁄₁₆ x 9 ⅞ in. (12.2 x 25.1 cm)

Inscribed lower left: *near El Areesh / 30
March. 1867. 3.30 PM*; lower right: *(27)*;
with other notations

BI1997.7.323

123 *El Areesh*, 6:30 pm, 31 March 1867 (33)

Pen and brown ink with watercolor
over graphite

3 ⅛ x 9 in. (7.9 x 22.9 cm)

Inscribed lower left: *El Areesh / 6.30. PM.
March 31. 1867*; lower right: *(33)*;
with other notations

BI1997.7.325

Returning down the Nile in late February
and early March, Lear traveled to Memphis
in the Delta and on to Suez and then to El
Areesh on the Mediterranean. As Wilkinson
related in Murray's *Handbook*, El Areesh
"succeeded to the ancient Rhinocolura,
which was a place of exile in the time of the
Pharaohs, and was so called from the male-
factors having their 'noses cut off,' instead
of being punished by death."[1]

1 Wilkinson, p. 210.

122

123

Pettinasco. Lago D'Orta. 4. PM. June 2. 1867   *(221)*

124

yellow

Lake

light

off

Lake

myriad fine stalks   threads   blue gray

Pettinasco. Lago d'Orta. 4.20. PM. June 2. 1867   *(224)*

125

124 *Pettinasco, Lago d'Orta*, 4:00 pm,
2 June 1867 (221)

Pen and brown ink with watercolor
over graphite
4 ⁵⁄₁₆ x 8 ½ in. (11 x 21.6 cm)

Inscribed lower left: *Pettinasco. Lago D'Orta.
4. PM. June 2. 1867*; lower right *(221)*;
with other notations

B1997.7.346

125 *Pettinasco, Lago d'Orta*, 4:20 pm,
2 June 1867 (224)

Pen and brown ink with watercolor
over graphite
4 ¼ x 6 ⁵⁄₁₆ in. (10.8 x 16 cm)

Inscribed lower left: *Pettinasco / Lago d'Orta.
4.20. PM. June 2. 1867*; lower right: *(224)*;
with other notations

B1997.7.349

Rather than continue on to Palestine after his
trip up the Nile, as he had originally intended,
Lear traveled to the Italian Lakes, visiting
Garda, Idro, Iseo, Varese, Como and Maggiore
before arriving at Orta on June 1, 1867. The
following day, after a hot morning of walking
and drawing, Lear lunched at Pettinasco,
then napped until 2:30. In the afternoon he
drew "bits of the beautiful foreground—rye
& vine & rock & fern" before hurrying back
to his hotel in advance of a thunderstorm.[1]

1 Diary, June 2, 1867, Manuscript, Houghton Library,
Harvard University.

Cannes, 1869

126 *A View of the Harbor at Cannes*, 1869

Watercolor with gouache and
scraping out over graphite
6 9/16 x 20 1/8 in. (16.7 x 51.1 cm)

Inscribed lower left: *Cannes*; signed lower
right with EL monogram and dated: *1869*

Paul Mellon Collection
B 1975.4.1930

127 *A View of the Pine Woods above Cannes*, 1869
SEE PAGE 32

Watercolor with scraping out
and gum over graphite
6 5/8 x 20 1/2 in. (16.8 x 51.1 cm)

Inscribed lower left: *Cannes*; signed lower
right with EL monogram and dated: *1869*

Paul Mellon Collection
B1981.25.2644

With the return of Corfu to Greece in 1863, Lear
lost his longtime base of operations in the
Mediterranean. He considered several spots as
potential winter residences, including Cannes,
where he stayed from December 1867 to April
1868 and again in the winter and spring of 1870.
He wrote to Lady Waldegrave in January 1868:
"Cannes is a place literally with no amusements;
people who come must live… absolutely to
themselves in a country life, or make excursions
to the really beautiful places about when weather
permits. I know of no place where there are such
walks close to the town: and the Esterel range is
what you can look at all day with delight.…
There is no fog of any sort."[1] The hard-edged
brilliance of *A View of the Pine Woods above
Cannes* shows the Esterel Mountains with that
clarity of atmosphere that so impressed Lear.

1 Letter to Lady Waldegrave, January 9, 1868, *Later
Letters*, p. 93.

126

128

128 *The Forest of Valdoniello, Corsica*, 1869

Oil on canvas
36 ⅛ x 58 ⅛ in. (92.75 x 148.5 cm)

Signed lower right with EL monogram

Paul Mellon Collection
B1976.7.52

Lear spent the months of April and May 1868 in Corsica. He was in the forest of Valdoniello on May 12 through 14. In the published journal of his Corsican visit (cat. 129), he commented on the vastness of the forest and noted: "No portion of this sublime forest landscape is more striking than the flat tops of some of the singularly Turneresque or Martinesque pines, relieving almost positively black against the great distance beyond." He was concerned about the ravages of commercial logging in the forest, but admitted that the process had its aesthetic benefits, at least in the short term: "It must be confessed that the very thinning of Valdoniello, which is preluding its downfall, has its advantages in providing space for light and shadow, for which there was no room in the close dense masses of wood before the work of destruction began."

129 *Journal of a Landscape Painter in Corsica*
London: Robert John Bush, 1870

Shown: Plate XIV, *Forest of Bavella*
Wood engraving

Paul Mellon Collection

This was the last of Lear's travel books and the only one to be illustrated with wood engravings rather than lithographs. Lear was not happy with the results, finding them "hard and hideous." Shown here is an illustration of the pine forest of Bavella, which Lear described in the text as "one of the most beautiful and wonderful dream-scenes of forest landscape it has been my lot to see." Lear included another view of the forest of Bavella as one of his Tennyson illustrations (see cat. 133).

129

Oil Paintings of India, 1879–1882

30 *Kangchenjunga from Darjeeling,* 1879
SEE PAGE 12

Oil on canvas
47 ⅛ x 72 in. (119.7 x 182.9 cm)

Signed lower left with EL monogram and dated: *1879*

B 1997.7.3

Invited to visit India by his friend George Baring, Lord Northbrook, who had recently been appointed viceroy, Lear arrived in Bombay on November 22, 1873. Over the course of the next year, he traveled throughout India and Ceylon. He arrived in Darjeeling on January 16, 1874. In his Indian Journal for the following day he noted, "Wonderful /wonderful view of Kinchinjunga!!!!"[1] Although the mountain would become the subject for three monumental oil paintings and several finished watercolors, his reaction to Kinchinjunga, as he referred to it, over the next few days was decidedly mixed. The following day he wrote: "Kinchinjunga is not—so it seems to me,—a sympathetic mountain; it is so far off— so very god=like & stupendous,—& all that great world of dark opal vallies full of misty, hardly to be imagined forms,—besides the all but impossibility of expressing the whole as a scene,—make up a rather distracting & repelling whole," and the day after that: "Kinchinjunga at sunrise is a glory not to be forgotten; Kinchinjunga pm is apt to become a wonderful hash of Turneresque colour & mist & space but with little claim to forming a picture of grand effect." Finally on January 21, he seemed to get the vision of the mountain that he needed: "Clear morning. Kinchinjunga altogether cloudless, & rosy as the sun riz,—but all & everything below the loftiest points was hidden by mist…. Near sunset, we were at the little Buddhist shrine,—a picture with Kinchinjunga clear & rosy=heighted beyond."[2]

Lear had traveled to India with a commission from Lord Aberdare for a painting of an Indian subject of Lear's choosing. Back in San Remo in 1875, he began work on the first of his three grand oil versions of this view of Kangchenjunga for Lord Aberdare. Lear sent the finished painting (now belonging to the Cynon Valley Borough Council) off to London in 1877 along with a second version that he had painted for Louisa, Lady Ashburton (private collection, U.S.A.). The version exhibited here was painted for Lord Northbrook in 1879.[3]

The composition includes the "little Buddhist shrine" that Lear noted on January 21, 1874, but the light is not that of evening. Lear avoids both the rosy glow of sunrise and the Turnerian mistiness of sunset in favor of the clear light of the middle of the day. Lear's annotations of the sketches he made while in Darjeeling (Houghton Library) are indicative of his sense of the oppressiveness of the jungle—"strangle tree" and "jungle-bungle / tangle jangle" are examples—above which rises the mountain range clean and pure. This contrast forms a basic structuring principle of the oil paintings.

1 Indian Journal, January 17, 1874, Manuscript, Houghton Library, Harvard University. Lear produced his Indian Journal in San Remo in 1875-78, transcribing his Indian diaries (also in the Houghton Library) into an album for Franklin Lushington, who later gave it to Lord Northbrook. In the corresponding diary entry, Lear used only one "wonderful" and three exclamation points. This heightening of response by the subtle alteration of the text can been seen at various points in the transcription. The Indian Journal entry for January 20, 1874 reads: "The mountain views are wonderful—Himalaya out & out;—yet I fancy at moments not so lovely as some I have seen in Greece,—barring the incredible vegetation here. Comparisons is odorous," which is rather more positive than the diary version: "The mountain views were wonderful quâ Himalaya, though not so lovely as those of Greece—barring the incredible vegetation."

2 All quotations from the Indian Journal, January 18-21, 1874.

3 A finished watercolor of a similar composition but with the figures and shrine on the right was sold at Christie's, London, on October 5, 1999.

131 *The Marble Rocks – Nerbudda Jubbolpore,* 1882

Oil on canvas

17 x 9 ½ in. (38.1 x 24.1 cm)

Signed lower right with EL monogram and dated: *1882.* Inscribed lower left: *Jubbulpour*

Paul Mellon Collection

L.1999-105.73

Twelve miles from the city Jubbulpore in the Central Provinces, the River Narbada flows through a gorge of magnesian limestone cliffs, from ninety to one hundred and fifty feet high. These are known as the Marble Rocks, and boat trips up the gorge were popular with visitors to the region. Lear visited early in his Indian tour on November 28 and 29, 1873. Both days he took a boat, sketching on the river. In his Indian journal entry for November 28, he noted: "Anything so powerfully and wonderfully beautiful in Rock scenery I never saw;—sublimely beautiful both as to colour & form & brilliancy—&c. &c. In returning by the boat which was quite easy in movement,—lo! No end of monkeys, evidently Entelus, bouncing and jumping about, or sitting on tree branches high up above the rocks & river. Black storks also. The monkeys were a delight. Such a loveliness of marbleism one never dreamed of."[1] The entry for the following day added: "The river scenery is truly delightful. More monkeys, calmly sitting,—unconcernedly on high rocks. Got several drawings, which may or may not be of use some day."

1 Indian Journals, November 28 and 29, 1873, Manuscript, Houghton Library, Harvard University.

131

Tennyson Illustrations

Lear met Alfred Tennyson in 1851, the year that Lear's *Journals of a Landscape Painter in Albania, &c.* was published. After their meeting, Lear sent Tennyson a copy of the book. Tennyson responded with the poem "To E.L., on his Travels in Greece." The two men became friends, although Lear felt closer to Tennyson's wife Emily. It was to Emily in 1852 that he wrote of a project he had been evolving:

> I think I once said something about illustrating Tennyson's poems—so far as the Landscape therein set forth admit of—. Many of the subjects I have arranged, though none as yet have I thoroughly carried out, which indeed it would require great time and labour thoroughly to do. But I have latterly extracted and placed in a sort of order all the lines which convey to me in the most decided manner his genius for the perception of the beautiful in landscape....
>
> It may seem rather impertinent that I can't help thinking "No-one could illustrate Tennyson's landscape lines and feelings more aptly than I could do"—but this very modest assertion may after all turn out to be groundless inasmuch as my powers of execution do not at all equal my wishes, or my understanding of the passages I have alluded to.[1]

Through the years Lear worked on choosing lines from the poems and selecting corresponding images from his collection of sketches. It was only in 1878 that he seriously began to work on the illustrations, intending to produce first 250, then 300, and finally settling on 200. Over the next few years he tried out different sizes and formats and considered different means of reproduction. In 1884-85 he produced one set of 200 small wash drawings, which belonged to the Tennyson family but were dispersed in 1980. A second set of 200 illustrations, drawn in the summer of 1885, are now in the Houghton Library. Lear died before he could bring the series to publication.

1   Quoted in Ruth Pitman, *Edward Lear's Tennyson* (Manchester: Carcanet Press, 1988), p. 27.

132   *The Pontine Marshes above Terracina,*
      c. 1880

Pen and brown ink with brown wash
over graphite
Image: 5 ¼ x 8 ⅜ in. (11.9 x 18.1 cm)
Sheet: 5 ³⁄₁₆ x 9 ⅞ in. (13.2 x 25 cm)

Inscribed upper left: *No. 8;*
beneath image: *"Stretched wild and wide*
the waste enormous marsh." / The Pontine
Marshes from above Terracina.

Paul Mellon Collection
B1975.4.603

At one point Lear took as the model for the
publication of his Tennyson illustrations an
autotype reproduction of Turner's *Liber*
Studiorum. This drawing, which illustrates a
line in "Ode to Memory," echoes the look of
the Turner prints.

133   *Bavella, Corsica,* c. 1880

Pen and brown ink with brown wash
and scratching out over graphite
Image: 9 x 14 ½ in. (22.9 x 36.8 cm)
Sheet: 11 x 16 ¾ in. (27.9 x 42.6 cm)

Inscribed upper left: *15*

Paul Mellon Collection
B1975.4.1317

Another drawing resembling the *Liber*
Studiorum prints, this one illustrates the line
"My tall dark pines that plumed the craggy
ledge" from "Œnone."

132

133

134

135

134   *Turin*, c. 1880

Pen and brown ink with brown wash
over graphite
Image: 10 ⅜ x 20 ⅞ in. (26.4 x 53.0 cm)
Sheet: 13 ⁹⁄₁₆ x 21 ⁷⁄₁₆ in. (34.5 x 54.5 cm)

Inscribed upper left: *9 / From the long alley's
latticed shade*; upper right: *Turin, (Italy)*

Paul Mellon Collection
B1975.4.1931

An illustration to "Recollections of the Arabian
Nights."

135   *Wady Feiran, Peninsula of Mt. Sinai*,
c. 1880

Grey wash with pen and grey and brown
ink with scratching out over graphite on
pale grey wove paper
12 ⅞ x 20 ¹¹⁄₁₆ in. (32.7 x 52.5 cm)

Paul Mellon Collection
B1977.14.6077

An illustration of the line "Imbower'd vaults
of pillar'd palm" from "Recollections of the
Arabian Nights."

136 *Mount Lebanon, Syria,* c. 1884-85

Pen and black ink and gray wash on wove paper mounted on card
3 ¾ x 5 ⅞ in. (9.5 x 14.9 cm)

Signed lower right with EL monogram; inscribed on mount upper left: *82;* beneath image: *A Cedar spread his dark green layers of shade / (The Gardener's Daughter.) / Mount Lebanon. / Syria.*

Paul Mellon Collection

An illustration to "The Gardener's Daughter."

137 *Areka Palms, Ratnapoora, Ceylon,* c. 1884-85
SEE PAGE 20

Pen and black ink and gray wash
on wove paper mounted on card
3 ⅞ x 5 ⅞ in.

Inscribed lower left: *Ratnapoora, Ceylon;* and signed lower right with EL monogram; on mount upper left: *65;* beneath image: *I will see before I die / The Palms and Temples of the South. / ("You Ask Me Why &c. &c.") / Areka Palms. / Ratnapooru. / Ceylon*

Paul Mellon Collection

An illustration to "You Ask Me Why."

136

Catalogue

PART TWO: British Artists Abroad

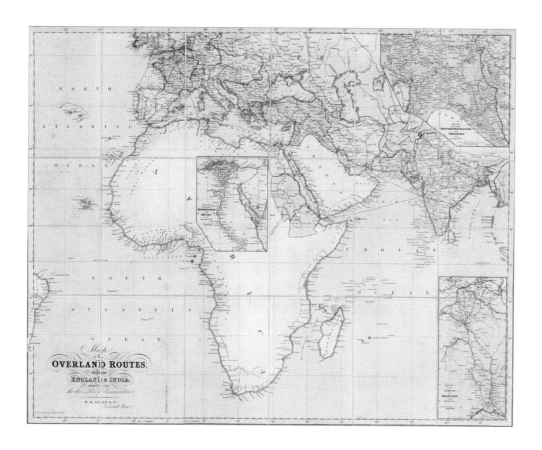

138 John Robert Cozens (1752-1799)
SEE PAGE 27

The Bay of Naples from Capodimonte, 1790

Watercolor over graphite on wove paper, laid down on original mount
14 ⁹/₁₆ x 21 in. (37. x 53.3 cm)

Signed and dated on mount lower left: *J. Cozens 1790*; inscribed verso: *Part of the Bay of Naples -*

B1977.14.6131

1 For the Cozens, father and son, see Andrew Wilton, *The Art of Alexander and John Robert Cozens*, exhibition catalogue (New Haven: Yale Center for British Art, 1980), and Kim Sloan, *Alexander and John Robert Cozens: The Poetry of Landscape* (New Haven and London: Yale University Press, 1986).

The artist, art theorist, and drawing master, Alexander Cozens, visited Italy in 1746. His son and presumably his pupil, John Robert Cozens, made two trips to Italy.[1] The first lasted from 1776 to 1779, during which time he escorted the connoisseur and antiquary Richard Payne Knight. On his second journey from 1782 to 1783, Cozens traveled with the young, well-to-do friend and patron of his father, William Beckford. Back in London, Cozens produced finished watercolors of Italian subjects based on the sketches he had made during his two visits. In this late work, one of at least three versions of the same scene, Cozens presents the view from atop Capodimonte (literally the "head of the mountain"), the site of the Regio Palace begun by Charles III in 1738. By 1794, Cozens had succumbed to serious mental illness and was placed in the care of Dr. Thomas Monro. An amateur artist and teacher, in addition to medical doctor, Monro acquired many of Cozens's drawings. Monro, in turn, made these available for study to his students, such as J.M.W. Turner (cat. 201-202). CD

139 Thomas Daniell (1749-1840) and
William Daniell (1769-1837)

Fakir's Rock at Sultanganj on the Ganges River, c. 1790

Watercolor over graphite on laid paper
21 ⁵/₁₆ x 29 ⁷/₈ in. (54.1 x 75.9 cm)

B1977.14.6141

1 For the Daniells, see Thomas Sutton, *The Daniells: Artists and Travellers* (London: The Bodley Head, 1954); Maurice Shellim, *India and the Daniells* (London: Inchcape and Co., 1979); and Mildred Archer, *Early Views of India: The Picturesque Journeys of Thomas and William Daniell, 1786-1794* (London: Thames and Hudson, 1980).

2 For the publication history of *Oriental Scenery*, see *Travel in Aquatint and Lithography, 1770-1860, from the Library of J. R. Abbey* (London: Curwen Press, 1957) vol. 2, pp. 372-377.

3 Quoted in Noakes 1985, p. 120.

Finding commissions increasingly difficult to attain in Britain, Thomas Daniell arrived in India in 1786, via China, with his fifteen-year-old nephew, William Daniell. The two would travel and work on the subcontinent for the next seven years, wandering all over India, covering the terrain marked out by aesthetic rival William Hodges as well as a number of uncharted regions.[1] This joint work of the Daniells appeared as plate x in the third part of their monumental *Oriental Scenery*, published in six parts between 1795 and 1807.[2] As with many of the Daniells' sites, William Hodges had been there first.

Differentiating themselves from Hodges's style, the Daniells show typical interest in precisely representing the holy shrine and carefully articulating the carving of Hindu gods in the rocks to the left. The Daniells also emphasize the intricate interconnection of the architecture and carving with the natural setting. The dramatic contrast of sunlight and shadow enhance the romantic and picturesque qualities of the scene. The watercolor is typical of the Daniells' work (both their watercolors and the aquatints in *Oriental Scenery*) in its subdued coloring. When Lear visited India, he was amazed at the brilliant colors, for which the Daniells' views had not prepared him: "How well I remember the views of Benares by Daniell, R.A. —pallid,—gray—sad,—solemn,—I had always supposed this place a melancholy,—or at least a 'staid' and soberly coloured spot,—a gray record of bygone days!—Instead, I find it one of the most abundantly bruyant, and startlingly radiant places of infinite bustle and movement!!!."[3] SV

139

140 Samuel Davis (1757–c.1809)

Chukha Castle in Bhutan, 1783

Watercolor over graphite
13 3/8 x 19 in. (34 x 48.4 cm)

Inscribed verso: *Chuka Castle in Bootan /
SDavis*

B 1977.14.266

1 Quoted by Michael Aris, *Views of Medieval Bhutan:
The Diary and Drawings of Samuel Davis, 1783*
(London: Serindia Publications, 1982). This book provides biographical information on Davis and a sketch
of British relations with Bhutan.

When Samuel Davis visited Bhutan, the British were consolidating their influence upon the territories surrounding Bengal. In 1774, the Bhutanese were forced to give up their claims to Koch Bihar in a peace treaty with the East India Company under General Warren Hastings. Hastings also won his demand for unrestricted British access to Tibet through Bhutan. In 1783 Hastings appointed Samuel Turner to head a mission to Tibet, with Davis, who had sailed to India in 1780 on the same ship with William Hodges (cat. 144), as the mission's "draughtsman and surveyor." Hastings later pressed for greater trading rights and a strict boundary classification, to which the Bhutanese eventually had to concede as well, though the concept of sharply delineated political borders remained foreign to them, as it was to many other indigenous cultures and societies in the region.

Davis's drawings of Bhutan combine topographical accuracy with the sublimity inherent in their Himalayan subject matter. Turner commended the drawings, writing: "His subjects indeed, in themselves, are not more remarkable for their grandeur and beauty, than for the judgement, fidelity, and taste with which he has seized on and recorded their features."[1] Nine of the drawings were engraved as illustrations to Turner's *An Account of an Embassy to the Court of the Teshoo Lama in Tibet; Containing a Narrative of a Journey through Bootan, and Part of Tibet* in 1800. Four had already appeared in Thomas Pennant's *The View of Hindustan* in 1798. William Daniell, who had spent twelve months with Davis in India in 1790-91, published another six, including this view of a seventeenth-century fortress guarding a trade route to India, as aquatints under the title *View in Bootan* in 1813.

After the mission to Bhutan, Davis remained in India, occupying a succession of civil-service positions until 1806 and pursuing his interest in Indian astronomy. He published two papers on the subject in *Asiatick Researches* (1790, 1792) and was elected a fellow of the Royal Society in 1792. His journal of the mission to Tibet was published by his son in the *Transactions of the Royal Asiatic Society of Great Britain and Ireland* in 1830. SV

141 Samuel Davis (1757–c. 1809)

Wankaka, 1783

Watercolor over graphite
13 5/8 x 19 1/4 in. (34.6 x 48.9 cm)

Inscribed upper right: *Wankaka*;
signed lower left: *SDavis*

B 1977.14.202

In addition to finished watercolors such as *Chukha Castle* (cat. 140), the group of Davis's works in the Yale Center for British Art also includes many working drawings in graphite and wash, such as this view of a monastery on the route to the capital at Thimplu, presumably done on site. The cache of Davis's water-colors and drawings at Yale, numbering 144 and comprising the majority of Davis's surviving works, descended in the artist's family until 1967, when it entered the collection of Paul Mellon.

140

141

142 Charles Gore (1729-1807)

Lago Maggiore and the Borromean Islands,
c. 1776

Watercolor over graphite on laid paper
6 ½ x 21 ⅜ in. (16.5 x 54.3 cm)

Inscribed across top: *Glacier St. Plomb[?] /
Isola Bella / Lago Maggiore / Isola Madre /
St. Bernard Glacier / Isola St. Giovanni /
Montagne di Lavino*

B 1975.3.163

1 An account of Gore's life, concentrating on his
association with Cozens and Knight, is included in
C. F. Bell and Thomas Girtin, "The Drawings and
Sketches of John Robert Cozens," *Walpole Society,*
vol. 23 (1934-35) pp. 8-11.

The Lincolnshire landowner Charles Gore resided in Italy from 1774 to 1778. A talented amateur drafts-man, he was, during his Italian years, the friend and traveling companion of John Robert Cozens, Richard Payne Knight, and the German landscape painter Jacob Philipp Hackert.[1] The Borromean islands, which lie in the west-central portion of Lago Maggiore in Northern Italy, provided a favorite subject for topographical artists of the period. A view of Isola Madre by John "Warwick" Smith is also in the exhibition (cat. 157). Gore shows the islands from a vantage point across the narrow lake, perhaps from the town of Cerro. While the work is not dated, a similar scene of Lago Fucino, grouped with this watercolor as well as thirteen others by Gore, is dated 1776. CD

143 Charles Gore (1729-1807)

Isola Bella, Lago Maggiore, c. 1776

Watercolor with pen and gray ink
over graphite on laid paper
7 ⅝ x 22 ¼ in. (19.4 x 56.5 cm)

B 1975.3.165

The terraced garden and villa of Isola Bella were built by the well-known Count Vitaliano Borromeo (d. 1690), for whom the Borromean islands were named. In the third quarter of the seventeenth century, the Count totally transformed Isola Bella and Isola Madre. On Isola Bella, he constructed the great villa depicted here with an ornate Renaissance garden consisting of ten terraces reaching over one hundred feet above the level of the lake. The terraces were replete with color from various trees such as cedars, magnolias, lemon trees and orange trees. On Isola Madre, he constructed a similar, though smaller, garden of only seven terraces. A larger version of this same scene by Gore exists in the British Museum. CD

142

143

144 William Hodges (1744-1797)

Select Views of India
London: Printed for the author, 1785-1788

Shown: *A View of Tombs at Secundrii near Agra*
Aquatint

1 William Hodges, *Travels in India, during the Years 1780, 1781, 1782, & 1783* (London: Printed for the author, 1793), pp. 122-123.

William Hodges traveled in India between 1780 and 1783, only five years after his return from Captain James Cook's second voyage to the South Pacific. The paths he blazed while exploring northeastern India would set the itinerary for countless British artists and travelers in the century to come. In March, 1783, during a lengthy expedition from Calcutta to Delhi, Hodges stopped in Secundrii to visit the Tomb of Akbar, the renowned sixteenth-century Mughal emperor. Akbar's tomb is shown towering above the trees, near the center of the print. Tradition held that the accompanying monuments housed the remains of favorite women from the Emperor's *zenanah*.

The lonely road at the center of Hodges's composition, along with the cracked, crumbling tombs which flank its sides, conveys the decline from the high period of Mughal power. Weedy plants and spindly shrubs have begun to break through the edifices, adding mossy patches to their once pristine facades. In his illustrated travel narrative, published ten years after his visit, Hodges recounted his thoughts upon reaching this once-sacred spot: "When the governors of this country were in plenitude of power, and exercised their rights with wisdom, from the excellence of its climate, with some degree of industry, it must have been a perfect garden; but now all is desolation and silence."

As was often the case, the sad decline of the Orient offered Western eyes a glimmer of picturesque beauty, which Hodges—schooled in the studio of Richard Wilson—was quick to seize upon. "A blazing eastern sun shining full on this building, composed of such varied materials, produces a glare of splendour almost beyond the imagination of an inhabitant of these northern climates to conceive; and the present solitude that reigns over the whole of the neglected garden, excites involuntarily a melancholy pensiveness. After viewing this monument of an Emperor, whose great actions had resounded throughout the world, and whose liberality and humanity were his highest praise, I became desirous of seeing even that stone which contained his crumbling remains."[1] SV

144

145 Thomas Jones (1742-1803)

Tivoli, 1777

Watercolor over graphite with gum
on laid paper
10 ⅞ x 16 ¼ in. (27.6 x 41.3 cm)

Inscribed upper left: *6/1777 at Tivoli
T. Jones / Tivoli – TJ 1777*; on verso:
for the painting

B 1981.25.2638

1   "Memoirs of Thomas Jones," *Walpole Society*, vol. 32
(1946-48), p. 60. For Jones, see also Lawrence Gowing,
The Originality of Thomas Jones (London: Thames
and Hudson, 1985), and Francis Hawcroft, *Travels in
Italy 1776-1783, Based on the Memoirs of Thomas Jones*,
exhibition catalogue (Manchester: Whitworth Art
Gallery, 1988).

2   "Memoirs," November 28, 1776, p. 53

3   "Memoirs," pp. 66-67.

Thomas Jones, a well-to-do Welshman, studied at Oxford before beginning his artistic instruction in London at William Shipley's School and the St Martin's Lane Academy. From 1763 to 1765, he studied under the renowned landscape painter—and fellow Welshman—Richard Wilson (cat. 160). Jones spent the years from 1776 to 1783 in Italy. There, he frequently sketched in the open air, creating fresh records of his immediate visual experiences, yet his vision was mediated by his experience copying the idealized images of Wilson, who was greatly influenced by the idyllic, Italianate paintings of the seventeenth-century painter Claude Lorrain. Upon arriving in Rome, Jones wrote: "I had seen and Copied so many Studies of that great Artist Mr *Richard Wilson*, which he had made here, and was so familiarized with, & enamoured of *Italian* forms, that I enjoyed pleasures unfelt by my Companions."[1]

Jones is remembered today not only for his watercolor and oil sketches, but also for his "Memoirs", based partly on diaries kept during his stay in Italy. The "Memoirs" provide an informative and lively record of the circle of British artists in Italy which included John Robert Cozens (cat. 138), William Pars (cat. 149), Francis Towne (cat. 159) and John "Warwick" Smith (cat. 157-158). Writing about his first autumn in Italy, Jones described his artistic practice: "I employ'd my self in visiting the Ruins, Churches and palaces— sometimes in Company and sometimes alone, for I could not always persuade my Counry men to attend me to see Sights with which they had already been glutted, and indeed the want of a Guide made me lose a great deal of time in wearysome and unsatisfactory perambulations...."[2] Jones visited Tivoli from November 9 to 16, 1777, remarking of the famous site: "At Tivoli—the foaming Torrents rush down the Precipices into the deep Abyss with a fearful Noise and horrid Grandeur—the immense Masses of Stone rise abrupt—luxuriantly fringed with Shrubs, and crowned with antique towers and Temples."[3] EB

145

146 Thomas Jones (1742-1803)

The Grotto at Posillipo, c. 1782

Watercolor on laid paper
Image: 9 ⅜ x 15 ½ in. (23.8 x 39.4 cm)
Sheet: 11 ¾ x 16 ¾ in. (29.8 x 42.5 cm)

Inscribed beneath image: *The Entrance,
near Naples, of the Grotto of Pausilipo –
which is about 2400 feet long,
in some parts 90, in others 70,
& in one part between 10 & 20 high*

Paul Mellon Fund
B 1993.9

1 Hawcroft, pp. 110-112.

Jones first visited the grotto at Posillipo in September 1778, near the beginning of a four-month stay in Naples. The grotto was a popular destination for Grand Tourists and a common subject for visiting artists. It was located beneath the tomb of Virgil and served as a passage, cut through the volcanic rock in ancient times, from Naples to Pozzuoli. Unlike William Pars and Francis Towne, who presented a more frontal view of the entrance to the grotto, Jones adopts a viewpoint to the left, framed by the edge of the monument normally seen in works of the subject. This use of the monument as a framing device was no doubt inspired by Peter Fabris's colored engraving of Posillipo in Sir William Hamilton's *Campi Phlegraei, Observations on the Volcanos of the Two Sicilies*, published in 1776.[1] Hamilton apparently loaned the book to Jones upon his visit to the artist in August of 1782, when Jones was again in Naples. Though Jones follows Fabris both in his composition and in the inscription, he pares down the scene to focus on the natural rock formations by excluding extraneous elements such as the oxen and horses found in the Fabris print. The monolithic rock wall, representative of the natural, even pastoral notions so indigenous to Virgilian pursuits, is the core of the composition, enlivened by the minutely detailed fissures and decorated with varied, lush foliage. CD

146

147 Jacob More (1740-1793)

A View at Terracina, 1778

Watercolor with pen and black ink over graphite on laid paper, laid down on original mount
14 ¼ x 20 in. (36.2 x 50.8 cm)

Inscribed on mount at bottom center: *A View at Terracina*; signed and dated lower right: *Jacob More Rome 1778*

B 1977.14.5480

1 P. Andrew, "Jacob More: Biography and a Checklist," *Walpole Society*, vol. 55 (1993), pp. 105-196.

The Scottish artist Jacob More arrived in Rome in 1773 and made it his home for the next twenty years, dying there only weeks before he was scheduled to return to Britain.[1] Known as "More of Rome," he gained great fame as a landscape painter. He specialized in views of celebrated Italian scenery treated in a classical manner modeled on the paintings of Claude. The ancient Roman hill town of Terracina lies on the Tyrrhenian Sea north of the Gulf of Gaeta. It was revered by tourists who knew of it through Horace's description (*Satires*, book 5, line 26). More divides his composition into three spatial and temporal zones: the background is primeval nature; the middle distance features ancient architecture; and the foreground contains present humanity in the form of fishermen. CD

148 Williams Pars (1742-1782)

Temple of Jupiter Pan Hellenius on Island of Aegina, c.1764-66

Pen and black ink and gray wash over graphite
11 ½ x 18 in. (29.2 x 45.7 cm)

Printed inscription at top center: *AEGINA.&*

B 1977.14.19425

1 See Andrew Wilton, "William Pars and His Work in Asia Minor," in Richard Chandler, *Travels in Asia Minor, 1764-1765*, edited by Edith Clay (London: Trustees of the British Museum, 1971) pp. xix-xlv.

In 1751 James Stuart and Nicholas Revett traveled to Athens to study and record the classical monuments of the city. They published their celebrated *Antiquities of Athens* in 1762. Two years later the Society of Dilettanti appointed Richard Chandler, a young classical scholar, to lead an expedition to Asia Minor to provide a comparable record of the remains of classical antiquity there. Revett was again to produce architectural drawings, and William Pars, a twenty-two year old portrait painter, was commissioned to provide watercolor views.[1] From September 1764 to August 1765, Chandler, Revett, and Pars worked in Asia Minor, spending another year working in Greece. The results of the expedition were published by the Society of Dilettanti in 1769 as *Ionian Antiquities*, with engravings after Pars's watercolors. Pars's finished watercolors became the property of the Society, which presented them to the British Museum in 1799. This less polished wash drawing of the temple now known as the Temple of Aphaia on the Island of Aegina was perhaps a working drawing from the expedition. It was included, along with aquatints by Paul Sandby after Pars (cat. 154-156) and watercolors by Willey Reveley (cat. 150-152) in a portfolio titled "Views in the Levant."

147

148

149 **Williams Pars (1742-1782)**

SEE PAGE 26

Temple of Venus and Rome, Rome, 1781

Watercolor with pen and brown ink
over graphite on laid paper
12 x 16 ¼ in.

Inscribed lower right: *Coliseo Rome 1781;*
buildings numbered *1* through *7*

B1975.4.1571

Pars first visited Italy in 1770 as an artist in the entourage of Lord Palmerston. He returned to Italy in 1775 to study in Rome with financial support from the Society of Dilettanti. For the last seven years of his life, he remained in Italy, where he was at the center of a community of visiting British watercolorists such as Francis Towne (cat. 159) and John "Warwick" Smith (cat. 157-158). His friend and housemate Thomas Jones (cat. 145-146) offered a poignant testimony to Pars's devotion to working from nature: he wrote that Pars died in October 1782 from an illness brought on by standing in cold water at Tivoli in order to sketch the Grotto of Neptune. In this watercolor, taken from a vantage point beneath an arch of the Colosseum, a Grand Tourist intent on taking in the sights of Rome surveys the scene, aided by a local guide. The guide points to the east end of the Forum and the coffered apse of the Temple of Venus and Rome, regarded as one of the most splendid Roman temples (also the subject of an early oil by Lear in the exhibition, cat. 21). EB

150 **Willey Reveley (1760-1799)**

Temple Ruins at Paestum, c. 1785

Watercolor with pen and gray ink over
graphite on laid paper
14 ⅜ x 20 ⁷⁄₁₆ in. (36.5 x 51.9 cm)

Inscribed upper left: *13*

B 1977.14.19454

1 See the entry on Reveley in John Ingamells,
A Dictionary of British and Irish Travellers in Italy,
1701-1800 (New Haven: Yale University Press, 1997),
pp. 807-808.

Reveley, an architect and draftsman, was already resident in Rome in 1784, when Sir Richard Worsley, a former politician turned full-time collector and connoisseur, engaged him as draftsman for a tour of Greece and Egypt.[1] They left Rome on February 12, traveling south to Naples and visiting Paestum between February 20 and 25. Paestum, located on the sea near Salerno, was known as Poseidonia by the Greeks who founded it around 600 B.C. The site became popular as the best example of Greek classical architecture on the Italian mainland after the famous antiquary Johann Winckelmann rediscovered it in the 1750s. The view rendered here is from the north, looking south at the three temples of Ceres, Peace and Neptune. Characteristic of his work as an architect and draftsman, Reveley uses fine pen lines to define the major compositional features, but also to evoke the ruggedness and antiquity of the architecture. CD

150

151 Willey Reveley (1760-1799)

Malta, c. 1785

Watercolor with pen and
gray ink on laid paper
10 ½ x 17 ⅞ in. (26.7 x 45.4 cm)

B 1977.14.19431

152 Willey Reveley (1760-1799)

Hagia Sophia, Constantinople, c. 1785-86

Watercolor with pen and
gray ink on laid paper
9 ⅞ x 18 ¾ in. (25.1 x 47.6 cm)

B 1977.14.19395

1 Wilton, *Cozens*, p. 52.

On March 26, 1785 Worsley and Reveley set sail for Malta. They would continue on to Greece, Asia Minor, and Egypt, returning to Rome by September 10, 1786. Although Malta would become a British territory in 1814, at the time of Worsley and Reveley's visit in 1785, it was still governed by the Knights of Malta.

This wash drawing shows the dome of the great basilica built for the Byzantine Emperor Justinian 1 in A.D. 537 by the architects Anthemius of Tralles and Isidore of Miletus. It served as the cathedral of Constantinople until the city fell to the Turks in 1453, after which Sultan Mehmet the Conqueror converted it into his imperial mosque. Reveley's drawings of Malta, Constantinople, and Paestum all come from a portfolio titled "Views in the Levant," which includes sixty-six drawings by Reveley, Pars, and other unidentified artists, and five prints after Pars (cat. 154-156). Although the portfolio has no known provenance before 1959, Andrew Wilton has suggested that it may have belonged to the Society of Dilettanti.[1]

151

152

135

153

153 Archibald Robertson (1748-1788) and
Paul Sandby (1725-1809)
after Pietro Fabris (act. 1768-1778)

Views in and near Naples,
London: Sandby and Robertson, 1777-1783

Shown: Paul Sandby after Pietro Fabris,
*View of the Ruins of an Ancient Edifice
on the High Ground of Baia*, 1777
Aquatint

1   The issues surrounding the publication of these views
    is set out in Abbey, *Travel*, vol. 1, pp. 140-142.

Paul Sandby was instrumental in introducing aquatint in Britain. His earliest published aquatints were of his own designs, *XII Views in South Wales* of 1775. Two years later he joined with Archibald Robertson to aquatint and publish a selection of Neapolitan views after Pietro Fabris, a topographical painter active in Naples who worked for Sir William Hamilton and other English patrons. It is unclear whether the twenty-four aquatints assembled in this volume, which bear publication dates of 1777, 1778, and 1782, were intended to constitute a set.[1]

154

154 Paul Sandby (1725-1809) after
William Pars (1742-1782)

Miletus, 1780

Etching and aquatint
11 x 18 ½ in. (27.9 x 47.0 cm) trimmed
within platemark

B 1977.14.19408

155 Paul Sandby (1725-1809) after
William Pars (1742-1782)

The Port of Aegina, 1780

Etching and aquatint
11 x 18 ¾ in. (27.9 x 47.6 cm) trimmed
within platemark

B 1977.14.19412

155

156 Paul Sandby (1725-1809) after
William Pars (1742-1782)

Entrance of the Acropolis at Athens, 1780

Etching and Aquatint
11 x 18 ½ in. (27.9 x 47 cm) trimmed
within platemark

B 1977.14.19414

Paul Sandby applied to the Society of Dilettanti in 1776 and 1777 for permission to reproduce drawings that William Pars had made during Richard Chandler's expedition to Asia Minor and Greece in 1764-65 (see cat. 148). Sandby published twelve aquatints after Pars's drawings, including seven — *Miletus* (cat. 154) being one — that had already been engraved as illustrations to the Society's publication *Ionian Antiquities* in 1769. Five of Sandby's prints after Pars are included with sixty-six drawings by Pars, Willey Reveley, and other unidentified artists in the portfolio titled "Views in the Levant" (see cat. 152).

157 John "Warwick" Smith (1749-1831)

Isola Madre, Lago Maggiore, c. 1781

Watercolor over graphite on laid paper,
laid down on original mount
12 ¼ x 17 ½ in. (31.0 x 44.5 cm)

Inscribed on mount bottom center: *Isola Madre Lago di Maggiore*

B 1975.4.1850

The son of a gardener in Cumberland, John "Warwick" Smith became one of England's most skilled watercolor practitioners of the late eighteenth and early nineteenth centuries. His work in Italy, which he visited between 1776 and 1781 under the patronage of the Earl of Warwick, is among his freshest and most lively. Together with other British artists in Rome, such as Thomas Jones (cat. 145-146), William Pars (cat. 149), and Francis Towne (cat. 159), Smith developed a naturalistic watercolor style. In August of 1781, Smith left Rome in the company of Towne, returning to England by way of the north of Italy and Switzerland. This view of Lago Maggiore is presumably a product of that homeward journey. EB

158 John "Warwick" Smith (1749-1831)

The Colosseum, Rome, 1802
SEE PAGE 24

Watercolor over graphite
2 ½ x 32 in. (52.1 x 81.3 cm)

Signed and dated lower left: *J. Smith 1802*

B1977.14.6287

1 See Timothy Wilcox, *Francis Towne*, exhibition catalogue (London: Tate Gallery, 1997), pp. 150-151.

In the years following his return to England from Italy in 1781, Smith made several tours of Wales and the Lake District, but his Italian experience continued to influence his work. Many of his drawings were engraved, including seventy-two plates for his own *Select Views of Italy* in 1792-1793. In 1806 Smith, now considered one of the grand old men of the watercolor tradition, became a member of the Old Water-Colour Society, which had been formed two years earlier. *The Colosseum, Rome*, probably the exhibition watercolor shown at the Old Water-Colour Society in 1807, is one of three similar compositions derived from sketches made during Smith's Italian journey.[1] Smith shows the Colosseum — ancient Rome's most famous monument and a popular subject for visiting artists — from the eastern end of Palatine Hill. To the left is the Arch of Constantine, and to the right two arches of the Claudian Aqueduct are visible. The ruins — partially overgrown with dense vegetation — allude to the passage of time and evoke a melancholy nostalgia for the former grandeur of the ancient Rome. EB

156

157

159 Francis Towne (1740-1816)

The Claudian Aqueduct, Rome, 1785

Watercolor with pen and black ink over graphite on laid paper, laid down on original mount
12 ⅝ x 18 ½ in. (32.1 x 47 cm)

Inscribed verso: *No. 4 a View of the Claudian Aqueduct at Rome / looking towards mount Palatine / Drawn by / Francis Towne / 1785*

B 1978.43.170

1 Edward Edwards, *Anecdotes of Painting*, London, 1808, p. 260; cited in Richard Stephens, "New Material for Francis Towne's Biography," *Burlington Magazine*, vol. 138 (August 1996), p. 500-505.

2 For a recent consideration of Towne's style as well as the fullest account of his life and work, see T. Wilcox, *Francis Towne*.

Francis Towne is noted for the spare linearity of his style, perhaps influenced by his seven-year apprenticeship (begun in 1752) as a coach painter in London. Edward Edwards noted the "sharpness of touch, which is peculiar to all those who have been bred coach-painters"[1] His interest in outline — at the expense of atmospheric color washes — made his technique idiosyncratic in his day.[2] He earned a living as a drawing master in Devon, to the detriment of his reputation in London, where he was often regarded as a provincial draftsman rather than a serious landscape painter. He traveled to Italy in 1780, spending most of his time in Rome and forming part of the artistic community of British artists in Rome that included William Pars (cat. 149) and John "Warwick" Smith (cat. 157-158). He returned with Smith via the Alps in 1781.

In The *Claudian Aqueduct, Rome*, painted following his return to England from a sketch done on site in Rome, Towne combines precise draftsmanship with simple washes of color to create an impression of crumbling masonry. Built primarily during the reign of Claudius (c. A.D. 40-50), the aqueduct was a popular subject for visiting artists. Towne emphasizes its sublimity with his low vantage point, dramatic contrasts of light and shade, and tiny figures at the lower left, giving the impression of a more overwhelming monumentality than in Smith's depiction of the aqueduct in his view of the Colosseum. EB

160 Richard Wilson (1714-1782)

The Via Nomentana, 1754

Black and white chalk and stump on gray paper, laid down on original mount
10 ⅞ x 16 ⅝ in. (27.6 x 42.2 cm)

Inscribed on mount lower left: *R. Wilson f. Romae. 1754*; bottom center: *The Via Nomentana*; lower right: *No. 18*

B 1977.14.4656

1 Brinsley Ford, "The Dartmouth Collection of Drawings by Richard Wilson," *Burlington Magazine*, vol. 90 (1948), pp. 337-45; for Wilson see also David Solkin, *Richard Wilson: The Landscape of Reaction*, exhibition catalogue (London: Tate Gallery, 1982).

The Welsh-born artist Richard Wilson studied under a portrait-painter in London beginning in 1729, and by the time he left for Rome in 1750 he had established himself as a portraitist and view painter. It was during his stay in Italy to 1756 that he became a painter of classical landscape, heavily influenced by the idealized Italian landscapes of the seventeenth-century painter Claude Lorrain. Through his own work as well as his teaching, Wilson played a large role in disseminating Claude's elegiac style within Britain. *The Via Nomentana* is one of a series of drawings of views in and around Rome commissioned by the second Earl of Dartmouth in 1754 through his agent in Rome, Thomas Jenkins.[1] It depicts one of the old consular roads just outside the city, with the Monti Prenestini in the background. EB

159

160

161 Henry Aston Barker (1774-1856)
Etched by C. Tompkins and
aquatinted by F.C. and G. Lewis

*A Series of Eight Views Forming a Panorama
of the Celebrated City of Constantinople*, 1813

Eight hand-colored aquatints

This set of aquatints records and commemorates the *View of Constantinople from the Tower of Galatea* that was exhibited in the Large Circle at the Leicester Square Panorama in London from April 27, 1801 to May 15, 1802. Robert Barker, who originated the idea of a large scale 360° painting in the 1780s and coined the term "panorama" to describe such a painting, opened his panorama rotunda in Leicester Square in 1793.[1] The Large Circle, in which the *View of Constantinople from the Tower of Galatea* was exhibited, was ninety feet in diameter and fifty-seven feet in height, accommodating a painting on some ten thousand square feet of canvas. The painting of Constantinople was based on drawings made on the spot by Robert Barker's son, Henry Aston Barker, who had, through the influence of Lord Elgin, obtained special permission to make drawings of the city—permission which, the Barkers claimed in their advertisements, had never been given before and might never be obtained again.[2] A janissary was ordered to attend H.A. Barker while he was making his drawings.

H.A. Barker took not one but two different views of the city and its environs. On November 23, 1801, the second view opened in the smaller Upper Circle. While the first view, which was still on display below, concentrated on the city, the second view was taken from the Tower of Leander at the entrance of the Bosphorus. These were the first views of a foreign city to appear at the Leicester Square Panorama, initiating a succession of panoramas of exotic locales that would continue to the close of the establishment in 1863.

1   For the history of the panorama, see Ralph Hyde, *Panoramania! The Art and Entertainment of the "All-Embracing" View*, exhibition catalogue (London: Barbican Art Gallery, 1988), and Stephan Oettermann, *The Panorama: History of a Mass Medium*, translated by Deborah Lucas Schneider (New York: Zone Books, 1997).

2   Although H. A. Barker in his publicity stated that permission to take the drawings had been obtained through Elgin (*The Morning Chronicle*, June 10, 1795), in the journal that Barker kept during his trip to Constantinople, he noted that on his first meeting with Elgin, "his Lordship took no notice of my business & very little of myself" (National Library of Scotland, MS 9647, p. 83). Elgin later did express interest in Barker's project (ibid., p. 84), but it was through a Mr. Spencer Smith and a Mr. Pisani that Barker received the order from the Porte to be admitted to the Tower of Galatea (ibid., pp. 86-88, 90-91).

162 Francis Bedford (1816-1894)

The Holy Land, Egypt, Constantinople,
Athens, etc. etc.: A Series of Forty-Eight
Photographs Taken by Francis Bedford for
H.R.H. the Prince of Wales during the
Tour in the East, in which, by Command,
He Accompanied His Royal Highness;
with a Descriptive Text and Introduction
by W.M. Thompson.
London: Day and Son, Ltd., 1865

Shown: Plate 27 *Mar Sâba, General View of*
the Convent and the Ravine of the Kidron
Albumen print from wet collodion negative

Beinecke Rare Book and Manuscript Library

1 Francis Bedford, "Some Hints on Landscape Photo-
graphy" *Yearbook of Photography and Photographic*
News Almanac, 1871, p. 27. For Bedford see Bill Jay,
"Francis Bedford 1816-1894," *The Bulletin of the*
University of New Mexico, vol. 7 (1973), pp. 16-21; and
David Hanlon, ed., *Commercial Aesthetics: Nineteenth*
Century British Photographs by Francis Bedford, Francis
Frith, James Valentine, and George Washington Wilson
(St. Louis: St. Louis Community College, 1992).

Francis Bedford, one of the foremost landscape photographers of the Victorian period, once remarked, "the life of a landscape photographer is assuredly an enviable one. The pursuit of his favorite art leads him to pleasant places."[1] Bedford, who had photographed treasures from the Royal Collection throughout the 1850s, was asked by Queen Victoria in 1862 to accompany her son Edward, the Prince of Wales, on his "educational" tour of the Middle East and Greece. It was the first Royal tour to be accompanied by an official photographer.

After the trip, 172 of Bedford's 8 x 10 inch prints were included in a presentation volume commemorating the Prince's trip. The photographs were also exhibited publicly, and their popularity led Bedford and his publisher to issue this smaller volume, containing forty-eight 4 x 5 inch prints with text by W.M. Thompson. In his introduction, Thompson praises Bedford's photographs for one of the chief values of the photograph in the Victorian period: "actual, positive truth."

Shown here is Bedford's view of the fifth-century convent of San Sabas, located in the Valley of Kidron. The monastery was a popular stop for tourists in the region and a popular subject for touring artists and photographers. Through his choice of vantage point, Bedford emphasizes the consonance of architectural forms with the natural rock formation of the valley. As Thompson notes, "it is often difficult to say which is natural cliff and which is masonry." MO

162

163 Richard Parkes Bonington (1801-1828)

Corso Sant'Anastasia, Verona, Italy, 1828

Oil on millboard
25 ⅝ x 17 ⅜ in. (65.1 x 44.1 cm)

B 1981.25.58

1 Quoted in Patrick Noon, *Richard Parkes Bonington: "On the Pleasures of Painting,"* exhibition catalogue (New Haven: Yale Center for British Art, 1992), p. 12. Noon's book provides the best account of Bonington's life and works.

Eugène Delacroix once remarked to his friend Bonington, "You are a king of your domain and Raphael could not do what you do."[1] Through a brilliant but short-lived artistic career based in Paris, the young Nottingham-born Bonington became an inspiration for artists on both sides of the Channel. After his death from consumption at the age of twenty-six he also became a type of the tragic romantic hero. Although he trained briefly in the studio of Baron Antoine-Jean Gros, his metier was not academic painting but landscape and *plein-air* sketching in both watercolor and oils. From 1822, when he left Gros's studio, he made frequent sketching expeditions in France and in 1825 visited London. He made his first and only visit to northern Italy from April through June of 1826, traveling with his friend Charles Rivet. From April 18 they spent several days in Verona, rich in literary associations as the home of an exiled Dante and as the setting of Shakespearean masterworks such as *Romeo and Juliet*. It was at that time or shortly thereafter that Bonington produced a celebrated watercolor of this street scene (Victoria and Albert Museum, London). Returning to the composition for an oil painting two years later, Bonington added a Catholic procession, which recalls a medieval world unchanged by the passage of centuries, a world of mysterious Catholic pomp and ceremony foreign to many English visitors. This work was still in Bonington's possession at the time of his death, and it is thought to be his last oil painting. MO

164 Thomas Hartley Cromek (1809-1873)

The Parthenon, c. 1834
SEE PAGE 33

Watercolor over graphite
14 ¾ x 21 ½ in.

Friends of British Art Fund
B 1993.35

1 Quoted in *Cromek: A Classical Vision*, p. 35.

In June of 1830 the Yorkshire artist Thomas Cromek left England for Italy. He traveled with his mother, who was going south for her health. For the next nineteen years, Cromek remained based in Rome and Florence, sketching throughout the peninsula and making a living by giving drawing lessons and selling his crisp, clear watercolors of Italian views to visiting aristocracy. In the summer of 1834 Cromek, with his mother, traveled to Greece. They spent several weeks in Athens, Cromek writing in his journal on August 23: "I was delighted with everything I saw at Athens, the colour of the buildings being much richer and less dark than that of the ruins in Rome. As specimens of architecture they are universally considered perfect."[1]

163

165 Thomas Hartley Cromek (1809-1873)

*The Interior of the Lower Basilica of
St. Francis at Assisi*, 1839

Watercolor and gouache with gum arabic
13 ⅝ x 19 ⅜ in (34.6 x 49.2 cm)
Inscribed lower right: *T.H. Cromek /
Assisi / 1839*

Friends of British Art Fund
B 1993.14

166

166 Edward Thomas Daniell (1804-1842)

Summit of Mount Sinai or Jebel Musa, 1840

Watercolor and gouache over graphite
on beige wove paper
13 ⅛ x 19 ½ in. (33.3 x 49.5 cm)

Inscribed lower left: *Summit of Mount Sinai
or Jebel Musa / June 20. 1840*

B 1977.14.4637

1   For E.T. Daniell, see Jane Thistlethwaite, *The Etchings
of E.T. Daniell* (reprinted from Norfolk Archaeology,
vol. 36, 1974), and Andrew Moore, *The Norwich
School* (Norwich: Norfolk Museums Service, 1985),
pp. 109-111.

The Rev. Edward Thomas Daniell (no relation to Thomas and William Daniell, cat. 139 and 167) was a talented etcher and painter associated with the second generation of the Norwich School.[1] After a Continental tour from 1829 to 1831, he became curate of Banham, Norfolk, and from 1835 curate of St. Mary's Church, North Audley Street in London. He counted among his friends many artists including David Roberts (cat. 191-196), Charles Eastlake (cat. 170), and J.M.W. Turner (cat. 201-202). Inspired by Roberts's watercolors of Egypt and Palestine, Daniell resigned his curacy in 1840 and set off for the Middle East. He was in Corfu by September, Athens by December, and Alexandria by January 1841. He traveled up the Nile to Nubia and then to Sinai, where he made this drawing on June 20. He continued on to Palestine and in December 1841 joined an archaeological expedition following in Charles Fellows' footsteps to Lycia, where Daniell died of malaria on September 24, 1842.

165

167 Thomas Daniell (1749-1840)

Ruins of the Naurattan, Sasaram, Bihar, 1811

Oil on canvas
38 9/16 x 53 5/8 in (98.3 x 136.2 cm)

B 1976.7.21

1 Pratapaditya Pal and Vidya Dehejia, *From Merchants to Emperors, British Artists and India: 1757-1930* (London: Cornell University Press, 1986), pp. 105-109.

2 Hodges, *Travels in India*, p. 16.

Like William Hodges (cat. 144), Thomas Daniell emerged as an artist from a humble background. Yet this bricklayer would soon impress all of England with his Indian landscapes, which eventually found their way onto Staffordshire blue-and-white porcelain.[1] Hodges himself commented in his *Travels in India* that many of Daniell's Calcutta views "are highly to be commended for their accuracy."[2] Daniell was primarily a topographical artist, often using a camera obscura to avoid the "inaccuracies" of Hodges's more picturesque renderings. Not to be left in the shadow of Hodges, he succeeded in amassing a greater amount of visual material on India than any other British artist to date. In 1799, two years after Hodges' untimely death, Daniell was named a full member of the Royal Academy, where he exhibited 125 landscapes between 1772 and 1830.

In this view, Daniell depicts a scene of perfect tranquillity among the Hindu monuments in Bihar, clearly adapting the tradition of the English rustic landscape to the Indian setting. Bihar was secured by General Robert Clive on August 12, 1765 through the Mughal Emperor's official granting of the *Diwan* to the English East India Company in the treaty of Allahabad. This district was soon after merged administratively with Bengal. The 1760s saw the Company build up a significant army for the first time as well as develop administrative agencies to control inland trade and to survey and regulate the activities of local textile producers. SV

168 Charles D'Oyly (1781-1845)

Mosque at Borranypore

Watercolor and gouache over graphite on gray wove paper
9 1/4 x 14 3/8 in. (23.5 x 36.5 cm)

B 1977.18.4

Born in India in 1781, Sir Charles D'Oyly was brought to London at the age of five. At sixteen, he returned to India as a civil servant for the English East India Company, where his work included such positions as keeper of records in the governor-general's office in 1803, collector of Dacca in 1808, and collector of government customs and town duties at Calcutta in 1818. Throughout, he cultivated his craft as an amateur artist, capturing the exotic scenes of daily native life which existed alongside the offices and factories of the Company.

As an artist, D'Oyly was directly influenced by George Chinnery, a portrait and landscape painter who resided in India from 1802 to 1825, before moving on to China and Macao. In Calcutta, Chinnery taught the essentials of his landscape style to D'Oyly, who then passed these skills on to a new generation of amateur artists. Like Chinnery, D'Oyly emphasized the peaceful, jovial scenes of village life in India. In this drawing, he conflates many of the images of rural Indian life into one harmonious portrait, offering a veritable cross-section of Bengali society. Native figures provide a variety of picturesque activity amidst lush vegetation, while a range of structures from hut to mosque suggests the various modes of native Indian architecture and living. The drawing was elaborated as plate nine in the posthumous publication of views by D'Oyly, *Views of Calcutta and its Environs*. SV

167

168

169 Charles D'Oyly (1781-1845)

Views of Calcutta and its Environs
London: Dickinson and Co., 1848

Shown: *Esplanade*
Lithograph by W. Robert and Lowes
Dickinson

1 For D'Oyly's publications see Abbey, *Travel*, vol. 2, pp. 422-423.

Charles D'Oyly set up the Behar Amateur Lithographic Press in 1828, and produced a number of books of lithographs bearing its imprint. This volume was published in London after D'Oyly's death.[1] This print presents a view of colonial Calcutta, the capital of British India. Located along the Hooghly (lower Ganges) river, the port city was founded in 1690, when the English established a small factory and garrison there. Fort William was built in 1696 and remained the center of the Anglo community in Bengal for two centuries, though as time passed, the British established a number of plantation-style homes outside of the large fort's walls. The town was constructed haphazardly and sporadically until 1803, when Governor-General Lord Wellesley introduced the first organized civic planning initiatives.

In a view reminiscent of contemporary depictions of imperial Rome, a blue sky filled with billowing clouds sets off a uniform set of white stone buildings built under British administration. The brown colors of the inhabitants and the dirt road and the unruly everyday hustle and bustle of Indian life in the foreground contrast starkly with the white-washed buildings in the background, which sit beside one another so closely that they form a veritable wall, displaying the strength and solidity of British rule, as well as its orderly aesthetic. SV

170 Sir Charles Lock Eastlake (1793-1865)

The Erechtheum, Athens, with Figures in the Foreground, 1821

Oil on canvas
26 ⅜ x 35 ¼ in (66.5 x 89.5 cm)

B 1976.7.26

1 Robertson, David. *Sir Charles Eastlake and the Victorian Art World*. (Princeton: Princeton University Press, 1978), p. 252.

2 Quoted in Robertson, p. 14.

Sir Charles Eastlake was an accomplished scholar, administrator and collector, a towering figure in the Victorian art world as both President of the Royal Academy and Director of the National Gallery. As a young artist, Eastlake traveled to Rome in 1816 and remained abroad for fourteen years. He produced watercolors as well as historical and genre subjects in oil, which he frequently sent back to England for exhibition at the Royal Academy and the British Institution.

Eastlake painted this view of the Erechtheum, a variant of a painting done the previous year for Frederick North, the fifth Earl of Guildford, as one of three pictures of classical ruins for a Mr. Devon in 1821.[1] Eastlake based the composition on sketches he made during a three and a half month visit to Greece in 1818. The Erechtheum, a third century B.C. marble building named for the mythical king of Athens, Erechtheos, originally housed the holy wooden statue of Athena Polias, the focus of the cult of Athena. In Eastlake's time, it was regarded as a perfect specimen of Greek architecture. Eastlake wrote from Greece that "I have no other object than the picturesque, and shall consider myself at liberty to put the mosque and the temple in the same picture, and to pay the same attention to the Turk's beard and turban, as to the bas-relief he sits on."[2] It is, however, conceivable that the presence in this painting of turbaned figures, oblivious to the grandeur of the monument behind them, provides not just picturesque incident but a comment on the Turkish occupation of Greece. Eastlake painted this picture in the year the Greeks began their war of independence against the Ottoman Empire. MO

169

170

171 John Foster (c. 1787-1846)

Temple of Theseus, Athens, c. 1811

Watercolor with pen and brown ink
over graphite
11 ⅝ x 18 ¼ in. (29.5 x 46.4 cm)

B 1977.14.4322

1 Quoted by David Watkins, *The Life and Work of
   C.R. Cockerell* (London: A. Zwemmer, 1974), p. 8.
   For the drawings by Cockerell and Foster in the Yale
   Center for British Art, see Pieter Broucke, *The
   Archaeology of Architecture: Charles Robert Cockerell in
   Southern Europe and the Levant, 1810-1817*, exhibition
   catalogue (New Haven: Yale Center for British Art,
   1993).

172 John Foster (c. 1787-1846)

Smyrna, c. 1812

Graphite and brown wash
11 ½ x 17 ⅝ in. (29.2 x 44.8 cm)

Inscribed top center: *Smyrna*

B 1977.14.4323

1 Watkins, pp. 13-14.

2 *Travels in Southern Europe and the Levant, 1810-1817:
   The Journal of C.R. Cockerell, R.A.*, edited by Samuel
   Pepys Cockerell (London: Longmans, Green, 1903),
   p. 136.

Born in Liverpool, Foster trained as an architect in London at the offices of James and Jeffrey Wyatt. In 1809 he traveled to the eastern Mediterranean to study classical architecture. In Constantinople he met another young British architect with a taste for archaeology, Charles Cockerell. They traveled together to Athens. In a letter of January 19, 1811, Cockerell wrote of his traveling companion and their accommodations: "Foster… is an excellent tempered fellow & as our style of life is entirely different we never clash, we have a house looking over the plain of Athens on one side & the Acropolis on the other."[1] In Athens, Foster and Cockerell became part of an international group of architect-archaeologists, who called themselves the *Xeineion* ("group of foreigners"). Over the next few years Foster and Cockerell and other members of the *Xeineion* traveled around Greece and Asia Minor visiting and excavating archaeological sites and making notes and drawings.

Late in 1811 Foster and Cockerell left Athens in company with the Hon. Frederick North and the Hon. Frederick Douglas to visit Egypt. After they had spent some time on Crete, North decided that the weather was not favorable and called off the Egyptian expedition. Foster and Cockerell decide to travel on to tour the classical antiquities of the "seven churches" of Asia Minor, mentioned in the Book of Revelation (Ephesus, Smyrna, Pergamum, Thyatira, Sardis, Philadelphia, and Laodicea). They arrived in Smyrna (modern day Izmir) from whence Cockerell set out for Pergamum, Sardis, Magnesia, Priene and Ephesus.[1] Foster, however, remained in Smyrna for personal reasons, as Cockerell related: "Foster has fallen in love and refuses to make with me the tour of the Seven Churches, as he promised, because he cannot tear himself away from his lady love."[2]

171

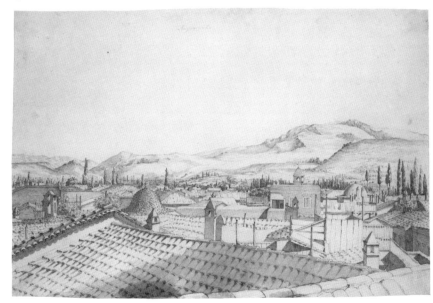

172

173 Francis Frith (1822-1898)

Egypt, Sinai, and Jerusalem:
A Series of Twenty Photograph Views
by Francis Frith with Descriptions
by Mrs. Poole and Reginald Poole.
London: William MacKenzie, 1859

Shown: *The Ramesseum of El-Kurneh,*
Thebes, First View
Albumen print from wet collodion negative

Beinecke Rare Book and Manuscript Library

1 Quoted in "Report," in Josef Maria Eder, *History of Photography,* translated by E. Epstean (New York: Columbia University Press, 1945; reprint ed. 1972), p. 234.

2 For Frith, see Kathleen Stewart Howe, *Excursions Along the Nile: The Photographic Discovery of Ancient Egypt* (Santa Barbara, CA: Santa Barbara Museum of Art, 1993); Kathleen Stewart Howe, *Revealing the Holy Land: The Photographic Exploration of Palestine* (Santa Barbara, CA: Santa Barbara Museum of Art, 1997); Stacy Miyagawa, *England to Egypt: The Photographic Views of Francis Frith* (Riverside, CA: University Art Gallery, 1988); and Julia Van Haaften, *Egypt and the Holy Land in Historic Photographs: Seventy-Seven Views by Francis Frith* (New York: Dover Publications, 1984).

3 The name "Ozymandias" was used in classical times for Rameses. It may have been derived from the ancient Egyptian name for the pharaoh, User-maat-Re. See Peter Clayton, *The Rediscovery of Ancient Egypt* (London: Thames and Hudson, 1982), p. 123. Shelley was inspired to write his poem after a visit to the British Museum, where one of the statues of Rameses from the Ramesseum was housed.

In 1839, the same year that Louis Jacques Mande Daguerre announced the invention of his photographic process, François Arago, a member of the French Academy of Sciences, suggested that photographers be sent to Egypt to record hieroglyphics since "the reproductions will surpass all others in accuracy and… will outshine the work of the most skillful painter."[1] Almost immediately both French and British photographers began traveling to Egypt, some on official government commissions, others as a commercial endeavor. This photographic interest paralleled both an economic interest in the region as a valuable overland route to India and an important source of grain, and a religious interest in the region as the birthplace of Christianity. Photographers and artists believed that they were visiting a land unchanged since the time of Christ.

In 1856, at the age of thirty-four, Frith sold a successful stationery business and dedicated himself to photography.[2] In that same year, he made arrangements for what would be the first of three visits between 1857 and 1860 to Egypt and the Holy Land. Motivated by the popularity of Egypt in the British imagination and his own Quaker faith, Frith hoped to provide the photographic equivalent of Roberts's popular work on the region. To that end he traversed the desert with more than a hundred pounds of photographic equipment. Travel photography in the Victorian era was a cumbersome and arduous process. Glass negatives were coated in a chemical emulsion and exposed in a large wood and brass camera for many seconds. They were then fixed and washed. As the technology for enlarging or reducing prints from a single negative had not yet been invented, Frith traveled with three different cameras to obtain three different photographic formats for his publications: an 8 x 10 camera, a 16 x 20 or "mammoth plate" camera, and a binocular stereoscopic camera.

Back in England, Frith exhibited his photographs publicly at both specialized photographic venues, such as the Liverpool Photographic Society, and more popular venues, such as the Crystal Palace. More importantly, he produced ten albums from his journeys, the first of which, *Egypt and Palestine, Photographed and Described* featured text written by Frith to accompany each image. In 1858, while Frith was still in the Middle East, his publisher James S. Virtue announced plans for a "sequel" to his first publication. This volume featured sixty prints with text this time not by Frith himself but by the sister of the Egyptologist Edward Lane, Mrs. Sophia Lane Poole, herself the author of *The Englishwomen in Egypt,* and her son Reginald, a member of the Department of Antiquities in the British Museum. The popularity of that volume led to the publication of the volume exhibited here, which features twenty mammoth plate (16 x 20 inch) views of Egypt and the Holy Land.

In the print shown, Frith presents Western tourists and their native hired servants at the fallen colossus of Rameses II in Thebes. The inclusion of these tourists could function as identifying figures for the home viewer or the armchair traveler in England. The colossus occupied an important place in the British public imagination as Ozymandias, the subject of the Shelley poem.[3] The warning "Look on my works, ye mighty, and despair!" is a powerful reminder of the contemporary conception of the fallen grandeur of the ancient Egyptians and the degeneracy of the modern Egyptians. MO

173

174 Francis Frith (1822-1898)

Lower Egypt, Thebes, and the Pyramids
London: William MacKenzie, 1862

SEE PAGE 35

Shown: *Valley of the Nile from the Quarries of Toura*

Albumen print from wet collodion negative

Beinecke Rare Book and Manuscript Library

175 John Fulleylove (1845-1908)

The Parthenon from the North End of the Eastern Portico of the Propylae, Evening Light, c. 1895

Watercolor over graphite with scraping out
10 ⅞ x 15 ¼ in. (27.6 x 38.7 cm)

Signed lower right: *JFulleylove*

B 1975.3.1017

176 John Fulleylove (1845-1908)

The Southern Side of the Erectheum, with the Foundation of the Earlier Temple of Athena Polias, c. 1895

Watercolor over graphite
10 ¹⁵⁄₁₆ x 15 ⁵⁄₁₆ in. (27.8 x 38.9 cm)

Signed lower right: *JFulleylove*

B 1975.3.1019

177 John Fulleylove (1845-1908)

The Castalian Spring, Delphi, c. 1895

SEE PAGE 36

Watercolor over graphite with scraping out
10 ⅞ x 7 ½ in.

Signed lower right: *JFulleylove*

B1975.3.1018

Frith took the glass-plate negative for this photograph in 1857 during his first trip to Egypt, and it is reproduced in *Egypt and Palestine, Photographed and Described,* his first publication. Criticism of that volume's lack of coherent geographical order combined with the popularity of Frith's photography prompted him to reorder his photographs of the region in a four volume series, to which the volume exhibited here belongs, published in 1862. Each volume contained thirty-six photographs with accompanying text by Frith and other authors.

For the photograph of the white limestone quarries in the town of Toura, twelve miles south of Cairo, Frith himself provided a mixture of fact and anecdote: "We have had a long weary trudge over that hot sandy plain; it is four or five miles across, and the rocks are steep and high… but we are amply rewarded by the view from the summit." MO

John Fulleylove's watercolors of southern France, Oxford and Cambridge, Paris, Versailles, Greece, the Holy Land, Edinburgh, and London constitute a late flowering of the topographical tradition. They formed the basis for a series of exhibitions and illustrated a number of travel books in the last decades of the nineteenth century and first decade of the twentieth. Fulleylove painted his watercolors of Greece, a high point of his work as a travel artist, during a trip there in 1895. They were exhibited at the Fine Art Society the following year and reproduced in *Greece Painted by John Fulleylove, Described by the Rev. J.A. M'Clymont,* published in 1906.

While Fulleylove's early watercolors purveyed an idyllic vision of the English countryside in quiet silvery tonalities, his travel watercolors are bolder in technique and brighter in color. At a time when the role of the topographical draftsman had largely been usurped by the photographer, it was specifically those aspects of color and painterliness rather than topographical accuracy that gave value to the travel watercolor.

175

176

178 James Duffield Harding (1798-1863)

Naples from the Strada Nouva, 1830

Graphite with watercolor and gouache
on gray wove paper
9 ⅞ x 14 in. (25.1 x 35.6 cm)

Inscribed upper right: *Naples, from the
Strada Nuova. / Nov. 26 / 1830*

B 1975.3.1026

1 For Harding, see Christine Swenson, *Charles
Hullmandel and James Duffield Harding: A Study
of the English Art of Drawing on Stone, 1818-1850*,
exhibition catalogue (Northampton, Massachusetts:
Smith College Museum of Art, 1982).

179 James Duffield Harding (1798-1863)

The Grand Canal, Venice, 1835

Watercolor, bodycolor, pen and brown ink,
gum and graphite on wove paper,
laid down on wood panel
30 ⅝ x 41 ¾ in. (77.8 x 106 cm)

B 1977.14.4411

1 This was published in *A Series of Subjects from the
Works of the Late R.P. Bonington* in 1830. Jane Bayard,
*Works of Splendor and Imagination: The Exhibition
Watercolor, 1770-1870*, exhibition catalogue (New
Haven: Yale Center for British Art, 1981), p. 72.

2 *Fraser's Magazine*, vol. 12 (July 1835), p. 55.

A pupil of his father, who was himself a pupil of Paul Sandby, Harding exhibited his first work at the Royal Academy in 1811, at the age of thirteen.[1] It was at about that time that he also took drawing lessons from Samuel Prout. Years later Harding and Prout would work together and eventually become bitter rivals. In 1824 Harding made his first visit to Italy. His frequent visits to the Continent in subsequent years provided the content of much of his work, both the watercolors he exhibited at the Old Water-Colour Society and the volumes of lithographs on which his popular reputation rested.

Harding produced this view of the Bay of Naples, during a trip to Italy in 1830. The largest city near important sites of antiquity such as Pompeii and the Greek temples at Paestum (see cat. 150), Naples boasted outstanding collections of classical antiquities as well as picturesque views. Harding's use of a colored paper with the highlights added in opaque white, a practice which he would advocate in his artist's manual *Elementary Art* of 1836, allows him to capture something of the brilliant effects of the sun in southern Italy. Following Harding's lead, Lear would employ a combination of graphite and white gouache on colored paper in his own drawings of Italy in the late 1830s and early 1840s. MO

Harding was elected an associate of the Old Water-Colour Society in 1820 and became a full member the following year. Hoping to become a Royal Academician, he resigned from the watercolor society in 1846, but, having failed to gain election to the Royal Academy, he rejoined the society a decade later.

Harding's view of the Grand Canal, exhibited at the Old Water-Colour Society in 1835, is an impressive example of the exhibition watercolor. It was based on sketches made in Venice the previous year, but, as Jane Bayard has pointed out, it also reproduces the view, looking down the canal towards Santa Maria della Salute, of a lithograph that Harding had made after a drawing by Richard Parkes Bonington.[1] At the time of this watercolor's exhibition, one critic recommended that J.M.W. Turner, who was showing his oil painting *Venice from the Porch of the Madonna del Salute* (Metropolitan Museum of Art) at the Royal Academy that same season, could benefit from studying this "exquisitely fine scene."[2] MO

In 1820 Charles Hullmandel, the leading exponent of lithography in England, printed Harding's first lithograph. The two artists would have a long and fruitful working relationship, producing together many volumes of picturesque travel and art instruction. Harding was in fact a popular drawing teacher, his most famous pupil being John Ruskin. Many of Ruskin's theories about art were formulated under Harding's guidance, although Ruskin soon sought to distance himself from Harding's aesthetics, stating of their drawings: "Harding's are all for impression; mine all for information."

Sketches at Home and Abroad was a pioneering publication for Hullmandel and Harding. Hullmandel had earlier introduced the practice of using a second tint stone to provide a colored background to the image printed in black from the primary lithographic stone. In the fifty plates in this volume, Hullmandel and Harding experimented with gradated tones and etching and scraping out highlights in the tint stone in order to reproduce the look of colored paper heightened with white in Harding's drawings.[1] MO

From 1831 Holland traveled regularly the Continent, and Continental subjects featured predominantly in his exhibited work.[1] Commissioned to provide illustrations for a volume of the *Landscape Annual* on Portugal, he toured the country in the late summer and autumn of 1837. The publication appeared in 1839 with a text by W. H. Harrison. Holland's watercolor sketches of Portugal (Victoria and Albert Museum) include one, dated August 26, of the Torre dos Clerigos ("Tower of the Clergy"), which was, according to Harrison, "one of the most striking objects among the public buildings of Oporto." Holland wasted no time in translating the watercolor into this oil painting. Although he had become an associate of the Old Water-Colour Society in 1835, by 1837 he was declaring his ambitions as an oil painter. He wrote to a friend: "I will henceforth devote myself to painting, and look forward with hope to do something worthy of note." In 1842 he resigned his associateship in the Old Water-Colour Society. Failing to gain the recognition as an oil painter for which he had hoped, he returned to the Old Society in 1856 and became a full member the following year.

At age seventeen, the Birmingham-born Johnson traveled with his teacher William James Müller to Lycia in Asia Minor. In 1874 he provided Müller's biographer with an account of their Lycian journey, noting: "Thirty years ago travelling on the Continent yet retained a spice of novelty and adventure, and was utterly different from what it has become in these days of universal steam and Cook's excursion tickets round the world."[1]

It is not known exactly when Johnson went to Spain; however, at this time, Spain was a popular destination for British artists as an alternative to Italy. Sir David Wilkie traveled to Spain in 1828, and David Roberts and John Frederick Lewis both made trips in 1832; other artists soon followed. Rather than focusing on the architecture of Moorish Spain or imagining picturesque vignettes of Spanish peasant life, Johnson here focuses on nature, producing a carefully observed study of exotic plant life. MO

180 James Duffield Harding (1798-1863)

Sketches at Home and Abroad
London: Charles Tilt, 1836
SEE PAGE 21

Shown: *Como from the Milan Road*
Lithograph printed by Charles Hullmandel

1 Swenson, p. 37.

181 James Holland (1800-1870)

Torre dos Clerigos, Oporto, Portugal, 1837

Oil on canvas
21 ½ x 15 ¼ in (55.2 x 38.7 cm)

Signed and dated lower right: *Jas. Hollland 37*

B 1974.3.9

1 M. Tonkin, "The Life of James Holland of the Old Society, 1799-1870," *Old Water-Colour Society Club*, vol. 42 (1967), pp. 35-47.

182 Harry John Johnson (1826-1884)

Aloes and Prickly Pears, Tarragona, Spain

Graphite with watercolor and gouache on beige wove paper
10 ¼ x 15 in. (26.2 x 38.1 cm)

Inscribed lower left: *Aloes & prickly pears / Tarragona, Spain. Sep 13th / Ecsavara y higos* [remainder of inscription cut off]; lower right: artist's stamp

B 1975.4.1299

1 N. Neal Solly, *Memoir of the Life of William James Müller* (London: Chapman and Hall, 1875), p. 203.

179

178

182

181

183 John Frederick Lewis (1805-1876)

Sketches of Spain and Spanish Character
London: F.G. Moon, 1836

Shown: *Distant View of the Sierra Nevada*
Lithograph by Charles Hullmandel

1 Though the two corresponded throughout their travels in Spain, their efforts to meet were continually frustrated. There is some evidence that a rivalry existed between the two and that their pictures were created in competition with one another. See Major General J.M.H. (Michael) Lewis, *John Frederick Lewis, R.A., 1805-1876* (Leigh-on-Sea: F. Lewis, 1978), pp. 16-17. This book remains the best biography of Lewis to date.

2 Quoted in Lewis, p. 16.

184 John Frederick Lewis (1805-1876)

*Main Entrance of Great Mosque (Ulu cami)
Bursa, Turkey*, c.1840-41

Watercolor and gouache over graphite
on brown wove paper
11 ⅞ x 18 ¾ in. (30.2 x 47.6 cm)

B 1975.4.1824

185 John Frederick Lewis (1805-1876)

The Ramesseum at Thebes c. 1850?
SEE PAGE 34

Watercolor and gouache over graphite on
beige wove paper
13 ¾ x 20 in. (350 x 507 cm)

B1975.4.1935

Despite his later travels and his famous ten-year residence in Cairo, John Frederick Lewis first gained renown (and the nickname "Spanish" Lewis) for the many watercolors and lithographs he produced during the two years he spent in Spain in the early 1830s. Lewis left England for Spain in 1832 and, proceeding via Madrid and Toledo, he reached Granada in September of that year. He remained there, sketching the Alhambra, until December, when he traveled on to Seville. In the following spring or summer, he left Spain for Cadiz, Gibraltar, and Morocco. His decision to travel to Spain may have been inspired by the trip in 1827-28 of the artist Sir David Wilkie, to whom Lewis dedicated this folio volume. In turn, he may have inspired David Roberts, who was to make his own trip to Spain a few months later. Both Lewis and Roberts were to publish volumes of lithographs detailing their journeys, for which they would both receive critical acclaim in England.[1]

In a letter of introduction carried by Lewis in Madrid, Richard Ford, a celebrated writer on Spain, called Lewis "a clever artist" and noted, "He is about to make a sort of picturesque tour of Spain, having orders for young ladies' albums and from divers book-sellers who are illustrating Lord Byron."[2] This image, the eighth of twenty-five plates, could have been conceived for such a project. Although titled *Distant View of the Sierra Nevada*, Lewis's image shows more interest in suggesting a subtle romantic narrative than in topography. EW

Lewis visited northwestern Turkey in 1840-1, en route to Egypt, and made a number of sketches of the local architecture. Bursa, located just south of Istanbul, inspired several pictures. Bursa achieved architectural distinction in the fourteenth century when it was the Ottoman capital. For its central business district, the Ottoman sultan Bayezid I ordered a new congregational mosque (Turkish *ulu cami*) which was completed in 1399-1400. Lewis depicts this famous mosque as an active place of gathering in the Turkish community. EW

During Lewis's residency in Egypt from 1841 to 1851, he made several excursions to Upper Egypt. This gouache drawing was probably made in 1850, when Lewis traveled up the Nile to visit Edfu, Luxor and the cataracts at Assouan. Lewis depicts the Ramesseum (also the subject of a photograph by Frith in the exhibition, cat. no. 173), which was the mortuary temple of Rameses II. Its huge statues and vast proportions were mentioned by several travelers in antiquity, but it was best known in Lewis's time as the site of the statue immortalized in Shelley's "Ozymandias." Lewis, however, was less interested in the impressive monument itself than in the landscape and people around it. In this drawing, the Ramesseum functions only as a backdrop, and, unlike David Roberts, who also drew this temple, Lewis exerts little effort in recording any of its hieroglyphic inscriptions. But if this is not an archaeological record of the temple, neither is it merely a picturesque study of Egyptian life among the ruins. As in many of Lewis's works, there is a narrative at work here, albeit a subtle one. The donkey and tent are not meant for the two Arab men, but for visitors to the temple. Their passive expressions and postures suggest that they have become accustomed to waiting for dawdling European tourists, who were streaming into Egypt in 1850 in ever-growing numbers. EW

183

184

186 John Frederick Lewis (1805-1876)

A Frank Encampment in the Desert of
Mt. Sinai, 1842, 1856

Watercolor and bodycolor
25 ½ x 52 ⅞ in. (64.8 x 134.3 cm)

Signed and dated lower right: *J. F. Lewis 1856*

B 1977.14.143

1   *Academy Notes*, 1856, in *The Works of John Ruskin*,
    vol. 14, pp. 73-78. The full title of Lewis's painting, as
    it appeared in the 1856 Old Water-Colour Society
    catalogue, was *A Frank Encampment in the Desert of*
    Mt. Sinai, 1842 – the convent of St. Catherine in the
    distance. The picture comprises portraits of an English
    Nobleman and his suite, Mahmoud, the Dragoman,
    etc., etc., etc., Hussein, Scheikh of Gebel Tor, etc., etc.
    The term "Frank" was commonly used in the nine-
    teenth century to designate any foreign traveler in the
    Middle East. Lewis exhibited an oil version of the
    painting (whereabouts unknown) at the Royal
    Academy in 1863.

2   En route, Castlereagh camped in the desert of Sinai
    for five days. He later recounted his trip in *Diary*
    of a Journey to Damascus (London, 1847). For many
    years there was confusion as to whether the Englishman
    portrayed was Lord Prudhoe, Duke of Northumber-
    land, or Lord Castlereagh. Rodney Searight put the
    argument to rest in 1979 with the discovery of
    Castlereagh's letter commissioning the work. See
    R. Searight, "An Anonymous Traveller Rediscovered,"
    Country Life, vol. 163 (May 4, 1978), p. 1259.

3   Letter from Casteregh to Lewis, May 10, 1842, quot-
    ed in Searight, p. 1259.

4   *The Works of John Ruskin*, vol. 14, pp. 77-78.

When this painting was first exhibited at the Old Water-Colour Society in 1856, the first year of Lewis's presidency of that organization, it drew effusive praise from the art critic John Ruskin. In his five-page review, he raved: "I have no hesitation in ranking it among the most wonderful pictures in the world," and commended Lewis on his unique ability to combine microscopic detail with compositional unity.[1] Lewis's remarkable picture is still ranked a masterpiece of the watercolor medium.

The reclining Englishman in the picture is Frederick Stewart, Viscount Castlereagh, who travelled to Damascus in May, 1842.[2] He is surrounded by his retinue, which consists of Count van Pahlen, Mr. Tardew (his physician), Mahmoud (his dragoman or translator), and two dogs. Scattered around the trav-ellers are various objects: newspapers, books, a map of Syria (titled "Ancient and Modern"), a bottle of Harvey's sherry, and a folding lounge chair. Standing before Castlereagh is Sheikh Hussein, Castlereagh's guide through this portion of the mountainous desert landscape, known as "Gebel Tor." The Sheikh is backed by a retinue of his own, which occupies the left-hand side of the composition. In the distance, placed exactly between the erect figure of Sheikh Hussein and the supine one of Lord Castlereagh, is the convent of St. Catherine.

In a letter to Lewis, written from Cairo on May 10, 1842, Castlereagh commissioned the artist to paint his portrait with his companions for the generous fee of 200 guineas. Lewis was free to decide upon the "place, persons, and details" of the picture.[3] Lewis had already made sketches of some of the members of the party while they were in Egypt and probably had sketches of the Sinai desert and St. Catherine's Monastery from a trip he had made just a few months prior. It is not certain, therefore, whether he actually accompanied the group as they set off for Damascus on May 23 or whether he composed the picture from existing sketches.

Despite the record of Castlereagh's request, Lewis's painting cannot be considered a straightforward "group portrait" or the commission a typical one. The picture was not finished until 1856, fourteen years after Castlereagh's initial request, and he did not buy it. There is the peculiar nature of the composition, as well, which seems to invite a symbolic reading. John Ruskin saw the key to the picture's meaning in the map of Syria, "Ancient and Modern," calling the picture "itself a map of antiquity and modernism in the East."[4] By this he meant that Lewis had provided a study in contrasts between the ancient, unchanging ways of the Arabs and modern (English) civilization. Subsequent scholars have also commented on the binary opposition set up in the picture, the clear right-left separation of West from East, and "culture" (marked by books, maps and newspapers) from Arab "nature" (camels and desert). However, the deliberate placement of St. Catherine's Monastery between the two central figures suggests another reading. At various times in the monastery's history, it operated as both a mosque and a church, housing the two religions peacefully side-by-side. This picture can be read not as the division or opposition of cultures, then, but as the possibility for harmonic union between them.

186

Though the watercolors of Egypt that Lewis exhibited in the years after his return to England in 1851 earned him great critical acclaim, he was disheartened by the lack of financial reward. He turned to oil painting in the late 1850s, and became a regular contributor to the Royal Academy. Although his travelling days were over, he continued to make Middle Eastern life the subject of his art. Writing to Lewis's wife in 1875, Lear commented: "There never have been, & there never will be, any works depicting Oriental life—more truly beautiful & excellent—perhaps I might say—*so* beautiful & excellent. For, besides the exquisite & conscientious workmanship, the subjects painted by J. F. Lewis were perfect as representations of real scenes & people. In my later visits to England, (& it is 3 years since I was here,) I cared to go to the RA. Chiefly on account of his pictures."[5] EW

5 Letter to Mrs. Lewis, June 22, 1875, quoted in Noakes 1985, p. 21.

187 William James Müller (1812-1845)

Karnak, c.1838-39

Brown and gray ink wash with gouache
on beige wove paper
10 ⅞ x 15 in. (27.6 x 38.1 cm)

Inscribed upper left: *6*

B 1975.4.1672

1 *Athenaeum*, August 18, 1838, p. 586.

2 William James Müller, "An Artist's Tour in Egypt,"
Art-Union, September 1839, p. 131. It is quoted in
N. Neal Solly, *Memoir of the Life of W.J. Müller*
(London: Chapman and Hall, 1875), pp. 82-83. Solly's
biography remains a major source on Müller's life
and art. A more up-to-date account is provided by
Francis Greenacre and Sheena Stoddard, *W.J. Müller,
1812-1845*, exhibition catalogue (Bristol: Bristol
Museums and Art Gallery, 1991).

3 Greenacre and Stoddard, p. 142.

Already by 1838, the year of both David Robert's and William James Müller's visits to Egypt, the temples of Luxor and Karnak were popular tourist attractions. The *Athenaeum* of that year regarded these monuments as "regular pieces of fashionable resort,"[1] made more accessible by improved steamship service between England and Egypt. Müller arrived in Egypt in November, just missing Roberts, who had arrived two months before. In January 1839 Müller reached Upper Egypt, where the temples of Luxor and Karnak made a deep impression on the artist. His diary entry of January 4 captures his romantic fascination with these monuments: "…to see Luxor [temple] in its full glory, in the same manner as our poet, Sir Walter Scott, has written of Melrose, 'visit it by the pale moonlight;' and it was in an excursion, or rather one of my idling moods, when, wrapped in my capote, I strolled through its deserted ruins, and had much pleasure in noticing how beautifully the colouring of the temple told (to use an artistical expression) by the light of the moon."[2] Müller's monochromatic sketch of Karnak temple evokes a similar atmosphere of moonlit contemplation. Ghostly white-robed figures are scattered amidst collapsed slabs of stone and are dwarfed by the massive columns that tower over them. Unlike Roberts (cat. 193), Müller eschews accurate archaeological accuracy in favor of broad romantic effects, referring to attention to topographical detail dismissively, as "taking medicine."[3] EW

188 William James Müller (1812-1845)

Near the Caravan Bridge, Smyrna, 1843
SEE PAGE 29

Watercolor over graphite
14 x 20 ⅝ in. upper corners rounded

Inscribed lower left: *Near ye Caravan
Bridge Smyrna / Octr.* 1843

B1991.35

1 Though this independence allowed Müller more artistic
freedom, it did cause him considerable irritation.
Many of the delays and difficulties that he and his
companion Harry Johnson experienced while traveling
were due to Fellows's broken promises and forgotten
offers of assistance. See Solly, p. 185.

In 1843, the archaeologist Charles Fellows suggested that Müller travel to Lycia (south-west Turkey) at the same time as his own government-sponsored expedition. Despite their initial contact, however, Müller's eight-month trip turned out to be a private artistic enterprise, financed by Müller himself.[1] Accompanied by his pupil, Harry John Johnson (see cat. 182), he arrived in Smyrna (modern Izmir) on October 4, where they were detained for a month awaiting permits from Constantinople. From Smyrna, they continued on to Xanthus, the ancient capital of Lycia, and camped for three months. In total, six large folios of drawings were produced by Müller while in Lycia and were shown, to great critical acclaim, at the Graphic Society upon his return to London in January 1845.[2]

Müller, in a letter published in the *Art-Union*, described Smyrna as "an ordinary Eastern town", picturesque only in the costume of its people. "But," he wrote, "the Turkish burial-grounds here are richer in their large cypress-trees than any I had previously seen; in particular those near the Caravan Bridge. There is much that is exceedingly poetic in these resting-places of the dead."[3]

187

2 In light of the popularity of his watercolors, it is interesting that Müller never published these works as
lithographs, in the manner of John Frederick Lewis or
David Roberts. The idea was clearly given some
thought, however. In February 1845, the *Art Union*
ran an advertisement for "Müller's work of Xanthus"
which was to include 26 lithographs from this trip.
Henry Graves & Co. promised to publish it in the
"manner of [David Roberts's] *The Holy Land*" (p. 33).
Though advertised again in April of the same year (p.
116), the folio never appeared.

3 *Art-Union*, February 1, 1844, p. 41.

4 [S.C. Hall], Obituary, "W.J. Müller," *Art-Union*,
October 1845, p. 318.

Despite the popularity of his works, especially the Lycian watercolors, Müller was dissatisfied with his treatment in the exhibition rooms. His unhappiness with the Royal Academy's hanging of his pictures led to a profound depression in April 1845. Although it was heart disease that brought his life to an untimely end just five months later, some contemporaries alleged a different cause of death. As one obituary had it: "We cannot hesitate to say that the Royal Academy as certainly killed William Müller as if they had stabbed his heart with a steel weapon."[4] EW

189 Samuel Prout (1783-1852)

Como, Lombardy, c. 1824

Graphite with stump and white gouache
on beige wove paper
10 3/8 x 14 5/8 in (26.4 x 37.1 cm)

Inscribed lower right: *Como*

B 1975.3.1072

1   W. H. Pyne, *Somerset House Gazette,* quoted in
    Richard Lockett, *Samuel Prout, 1783-1852* (London:
    Batsford, 1985), p. 65. Lockett's is the best modern
    account of Prout's life and work.

190 Samuel Prout (1783-1852)

Sketches in France, Switzerland and Italy
London: Hodgson and Graves, 1839
SEE PAGE 20

Shown: *The Forum, Rome*
Lithograph by Charles Hullmandel

1   Lockett, p. 60.

2   Ibid., p. 74.

Prout made the first of his many Continental tours in 1819, visiting Le Havre, Rouen and Paris. Almost overnight his art shifted from picturesque views of the English coast and countryside to equally picturesque treatments of the monuments and landscape of Continental Europe. In the 1820s he led the way in the popularization of Continental scenery and architecture both in the exhibition rooms and in the bookshops. He regularly contributed watercolors of European subjects to the exhibitions of the Old Water-Colour Society at a time when they stood out against "the endless repetitions of Tintern Abbey"[1] and published the drawings from his tours in a series of large format volumes of lithographs as well as in the more modest *Landscape Annuals.*

This view of Como probably dates from Prout's tour of Switzerland and Italy in 1824. While his later lithographs and watercolors could be mannered and formulaic, Prout shows a sensitivity to line and atmosphere which would set a standard for the travel artists of the succeeding generation.

Although Prout may have made another visit to Venice in 1827, most of the Italian subjects which he continued to exhibit at the Old Water-Colour Society to the end of his life seem to have been derived from drawings made on his tour of 1824.[1] That would also be the case with the Italian subjects included in this publication. A volume of Italian or specifically Venetian drawings may have been projected shortly after the 1824 tour; in 1833 Prout expected to be engaged for an Italian volume of the *Landscape Annual* (the job went to J. D. Harding); and Prout's correspondence indicates that in 1834 he was planning a volume covering scenery from Geneva to Rome.[2] However, it was not until this volume of 1839 that any of Prout's Italian views appeared in print.

189

191 David Roberts (1796-1864)

The Mosque at Cordova, 1833

Watercolor with gouache and some gum over graphite on gray wove paper.
9 ¾ x 13 ¾ in. (24.8 x 34.9 cm)

Signed and dated lower left: *David Roberts. 1833*

B 1975.4.1368

1   W. M. Thackeray, *Critical Papers on Art*, 1904, p.272 (London, first edition. 1850).

2   Unknown author in *The Gallery of Modern British Artists* (London: 1835) quoted in Michael Pidgley, "Travel, Topography, and Prints," in Helen Guiterman and Briony Llewellyn, *David Roberts*, exhibition catalogue (London: Barbican Art Gallery, 1986), p. 47.

3   Quoted in Francina Irwin, "David Roberts in Spain," in *Artist Adventurer David Roberts, 1796-1864* (Edinburgh: Scottish Arts Council, 1981), p. 12.

4   Quoted in Irwin, p. 12.

"He has sketched the spires of Antwerp, the peaks of Lebanon, the rocks of Calton Hill, the towers and castles that rise by the Rhine, the airy Cairo minarets, the solemn Pyramids and vast Theban columns, and the huts under the date trees along the banks of the Nile."[1] The novelist William Makepeace Thackeray thus characterized the career of David Roberts. Although the Scottish painter began his career as a painter of dioramas, panoramas, and stage sets, he is remembered today for his oil paintings, watercolors, and lithographs of locales from Edinburgh to Egypt. Roberts exhibited his first easel painting in London in 1824, but did not give up his theatrical work until 1830, when he decided to travel in search of architectural and picturesque subject matter. According to one contemporary critic, he added "a degree of taste and feeling" to his works that raised them above simple "elevations."[2]

Roberts set out for Spain in 1832. While countless other artists scoured the Italian landscape for picturesque views, Roberts chose to tap into the increasing public interest in things Spanish. The exhibition of Sir David Wilkie's Spanish views at the Royal Academy in 1829 had generated considerable popular interest. Writers and artists of the Protestant north were attracted to the mysterious and romantic Catholic culture with, as the American novelist and diplomat Washington Irving put it, "a dash of that Arabian spice that pervades everything in Spain."[3] Spain was, in the cultural terms of the period, an Oriental culture on the Continent. As such, it became an important stepping stone for artists such Roberts and John Frederick Lewis, who would both eventually work in Egypt and the Holy Land.

Roberts reached Cordova early in his trip, after sojourns in Burgos and Madrid. The city presented him with his first experience of Moorish architecture, which according to Roberts, put him "in a new world."[4] According to legend, the first mosque in Cordova shared a building with the Christian monastery of St. Vincent, thus the building was a powerful symbol of the blending of exotic traditions, both Catholic and Islamic. While the composition focuses on the "Moorish" arches, the column capitals of the side aisles betray the structure's non-Islamic roots. Roberts conveys a sense of the light and space of the mosque through the use of carefully modulated washes. The figures give both a sense of scale and the "local color" so important to the traveling artist. MO

192 David Roberts (1796-1864)

Picturesque Sketches in Spain
London: Hodgson and Graves, 1837
SEE PAGE 22

Shown: *Tower of Comares, the Fortress of Alhambra*
Lithograph printed by Charles Hullmandel

Roberts's publication of his Spanish watercolors as lithographs in his *Picturesque Sketches in Spain* contributed to the popularization of Spanish culture in the mind of the British viewer while enhancing his own popularity and reputation. Not surprisingly, he was elected an associate of the Royal Academy in 1838. While a number of the illustrations in the volume were drawn on stone by other artists, such as Thomas Allom, Thomas Shotter Boys, and Louis Haghe, Roberts did the drawing on stone for this particular lithograph himself. MO

191

193 David Roberts (1796-1864)

The Great Temple of Amon Karnak, the Hypostyle Hall, 1838

SEE PAGE 34

Watercolor and gouache with scratching out over graphite on beige wove paper

B1975.4.1579

1   For a full account of the complicated publication history of the work, see Abbey, *Travel*, vol. 2, pp. 334-41.

During his sojourn in Spain, Roberts traveled to Morocco, his first experience with non-European Islamic culture. This encounter inspired him to tour the Near East in 1838. Roberts arrived in Alexandria in September of 1838 and continued to Cairo and onwards to the Second Cataract of the Nile, stopping at the ancient sites of Dendera, Luxor, Karnak, Esna, Edfu, Kom Ombo, Philae, and Abu Simbel in succession. Roberts then returned to Cairo, sketching along the way at some of the same sites he had visited the previous month. Continuing on to the Holy Land, he arrived in Jerusalem on Easter of 1839. Back in London by July, he arranged with F. G. Moon to publish an illustrated book of his eastern views and organized exhibitions of his watercolor sketches in London, Edinburgh and elsewhere to promote the forthcoming book. *The Holy Land, Syria, Idumea, Arabia, Egypt and Nubia*, consisting of 248 tinted lithographs by Louis Haghe after watercolors by Roberts and a commentary by William Brockedon, appeared in parts from 1842 to 1849. The first section, *The Holy Land and Palestine*, was published between 1842 and 1845.[1] The lithograph based on this watercolor of Karnak was published as plate 57 of the second section, *Egypt and Nubia*, in 1849.

The Great Temple at Karnak is the world's largest extant religious edifice. The French explorer Champollion wrote, after visiting Karnak during his travels in Egypt in 1828-1830, "No ancient or modern people have thought of art or architecture on such a sublime scale, so vast, so grandiose, as the ancient Egyptians. They thought in terms of men a hundred feet tall." The hypostyle hall, so named because its roof rests on a row of columns, was the temple's most magnificent feature. Twelve central columns each twelve feet in diameter form two rows, creating a hall eight stories high with three aisles. Roberts depicts the view down the center aisle of the hall, indicating the scale of the columns through the tiny figures in native dress. These figures also serve to contrast the insignificance of contemporary Islamic Egypt with the grandeur of ancient Egypt, a contrast often articulated in Brockedon's text (see cat. 195). MO

194 David Roberts (1796-1864)

View of Kom Ombo, 1838

Watercolor and bodycolor, over graphite on heavy wove paper laid down on contemporary mount
12 ¹⁵⁄₁₆ x 19 ⁵⁄₁₆ in. (32.9 x 49.1 cm)

Inscribed lower left: *Koum Ombo / Novr 21st 1838*; signed lower right: *David Roberts. R.A.*

B 1977.14.6252

The temple in the ancient city of Kom Ombo is a binary structure devoted primarily to the worship of two gods. The traditional patron of the Pharoahs, the falcon-headed Horus the Great shared the sanctuary with the locally powerful crocodile god Sebek, whose descendents were often seen lurking on the banks of the nearby Nile. Because of its dual deities, the temple featured a double gate, a double entrance, and a double shrine.

Roberts gives the viewer no indication of the temple's unusual binary nature, little of which was evident before systematic excavations began in 1893. This watercolor gives a sense of Roberts working on site, with the general sketching of the hieroglyphics on the temple pediment complemented by the more careful drawing of the same inscriptions in the upper right hand corner. The lithograph based on this drawing was published in 1846 as plate 6 of *Egypt and Nubia*. MO

194

195 David Roberts (1796-1864)

From under the Portico of the Temple of Edfu, Upper Egypt, 1846

Watercolor and gouache over graphite on beige wove paper
13 ¹¹⁄₁₆ x 19 ¾ in. (34.8 x 50.2 cm)

Inscribed lower left: *from Under the Portico of The Temple of Edfou Upper Egypt*; signed and dated lower right: *David Roberts. R.A. 1846.*

B 1977.14.4377

Edfu in Upper Egypt boasted the Temple of Horus, one of the best preserved monuments of ancient Egypt. The god Horus was a divine metaphor for the living king, who, having vanquished the enemy, ruled as the victorious winged sun disc. The motif is immediately apparent in Roberts's watercolor as the motif spanning the central entryway to the temple. Roberts painted this watercolor in the Isle of Wight in the summer of 1846, as he worked to prepare finished drawings for the *Egypt and Nubia* section of his great work. *View from under the Portico of the Temple of Edfou, Upper Egypt* appeared as plate 32.

Roberts reveals his origins as a painter for theater in the way the portico frames the composition and in the dramatic poses of two figures on the left side of composition, whose gestures seem indicative of some unknown narrative. On the left a merchant seems to be displaying his wares. William Brockedon, who wrote the text that accompanied the lithographs, commented upon the interaction between ancient and modern Egypt in the Temple of Edfu: "In striking contrast with the magnificence of the ruins are the wretched huts of the inhabitants of Edfou… their miserable dwellings are stuck on every accessible place in and about the temple." MO

196 David Roberts (1796-1864)

The Hypostyle Hall of the Great Temple at Abu Simbel, Egypt, 1849

Oil on panel
14 ½ x 21 ½ in (36.8 x 54.6 cm)

B 1981.25.534

1 Noted by Roberts as nos. 142 and 143 in his *Record Books*, vol. 1, Yale Center for British Art, Save 1836 (MS octavo)

Roberts reached Abu Simbel on November 9, 1838, the last stop on his tour through Egypt, approaching the site on the voyage upstream from First Cataract of the Nile. The lithograph of the interior of the temple, which contains fewer figures, was published as plate 14 of *Egypt and Nubia* in 1846. Roberts painted the oil version as one of a pair for a Mr. Fouceareau; the other was a version of the interior of the mosque at Cordova (see cat. 191). The price for the two, without frames, was one hundred guineas.[1]

The shifting sands of the desert hid this temple and other surrounding structures for many centuries until 1817, when for fifteen days the engineer and amateur Egyptologist Giovanni Belzoni and three Englishmen shifted fifty feet of sand to create an entrance. Belzoni and his men, the first to enter the temple since antiquity took home souvenirs, two hawk-headed sphinxes, now in the collection of the British Museum. In Roberts's composition, tiny native figures serve as indicators of the sublime scale of the monumental sculpture. Their inclusion may also be a comment on the vogue for "souvenirs" from Egypt, as they appear to haggle over a mummy. MO

195

196

197 William Simpson (1823-1899)

The River Chenab, Punjab, 1865
Watercolor and gouache over graphite
14 ⅜ x 20 ½ in. (36.5 x 52.1 cm)

Inscribed lower left: *The River Chenab,
Punjab*; signed and dated lower right:
Wm. Simpson / 1865

B 1975.3.257

1   The best account of Simpson's remarkable life is
provided by Simpson himself, *The Autobiography of
William Simpson, R.I.*, ed. George Eyre-Todd
(London: T. Fisher Unwin, 1903). See also Mildred
Archer, *Visions of India: the Sketchbooks of William
Simpson, 1859-1862* (Topsfield, MA: Salem House,
1986); and *Mr. Simpson of the Illustrated London
News, Pioneer War Artist, 1823-1899*, exhibition cata-
logue (London: Fine Art Society, 1987).

The first war artist-correspondent, a scholar of eastern religions, linguist, journalist, archaeologist, and historian, William Simpson was also an accomplished watercolorist.[1] Raised in a Glasgow slum with little formal education, Simpson was an auto-didact. He left Glasgow in 1851 after an apprenticeship at a lithographic office and found work in London producing views of the Great Exhibition for the lithographic firm of Day and Sons. Asked by the publisher Colnaghi to go to the Crimea to record the war, he produced *The Seat of the War in the East* in 1855. The success of that publication encouraged Day and Sons to send Simpson to India following the Indian Uprising of 1857 to produce a mammoth illustrated volume on India. From October 1859 to February 1862 Simpson traveled throughout India, and after his return to London he spent several more years working up his sketches into 250 finished watercolors, of which *The River Chenab, Punjab* is one. Unfortunately, Day and Sons went bankrupt before the book could be published.

British India annexed eastern Punjab in 1846 after the first Sikh War and, in 1849, annexed Western Punjab. The newly-acquired Punjabi state proved invaluable to the British during the 1857 Indian Uprising, both by remaining internally stable during the conflict and by helping to reimpose British authority over the rebelling provinces in northeastern India. In 1859, Delhi was placed under the newly-formed Punjab administration in recognition of the region's loyalty to the British. In this image, traffic moves along a wooden bridge at a shallow bend in the meandering Chenab river. The foreground is littered with the abandoned tools of everyday work and living—a hammer, fire stove, wooden planks—while in the distance the mountains of Central Asia loom. Save for the bridge traffic, the landscape seems remote, lifeless and barren. SV

The River Chenab, Punjab.

197

198 William Simpson (1823-1899)

*The Blessing of the Suez Canal,
November 16, 1869*

Graphite and brown wash
on beige wove paper
10 ⅞ x 17 ¼ in. (27.6 x 43.8 cm)

Inscribed lower left: *The Blessing of the
Canal, 16 Nov. 1869 / Port Said. Suez Canal*;
with other notations

B 1986.29.550

1   The British, strongly opposed to French influence in
Egypt, had long frowned on the canal project, but,
after recognizing its importance for their own trade
with India, sentiment changed. Simpson's visual record
was produced in direct response to this reversal of
opinion.

2   Quoted in Pauline Rohatgi and Pheroza Godrej,
eds., *Under the Indian Sun: British Landscape Artists*
(Bombay: Marg Publications, 1995), pp. 144-146.

199   After William Simpson (1823-1899)

*Opening of the Suez Canal:
Blessing the Canal at Port Said, in
Presence of the Imperial and Royal Visitors,
December 11, 1869*

Wood engraving

Illustrated London News, vol. 55 (1869),
pp. 588-589

In 1866, Simpson was appointed "Special Artist" to the *Illustrated London News*. He travelled to Moscow, Abyssinia (now Ethiopia), India and Jerusalem in order to document royal tours, archaeological expeditions and other newsworthy events. The sketch seen here is one of hundreds Simpson made in 1869 while recording both the Prince and Princess of Wales's visit through Egypt and the opening of the new trade route to India. The latter was dependent on the Suez Canal, an immense and costly project headed by M. Ferdinand de Lesseps of France.[1] The Canal's opening was an impressive affair, attended by important personages "of every European nation". The ceremonies lasted for four days, from November 16 until November 20. Simpson illustrates an event which took place on the first day. It was described in the *Illustrated London News* as "the religious ceremony of pronouncing a benediction upon the canal, by the clergy of the Mohammedan, Greek Catholic, Coptic and Roman Catholic Communions, this once joined in praying for a single object." Exhibited are both Simpson's on-the-spot sketch, annotated to guide his professional colleagues in London who would have transformed the loose sketch into a detailed wood engraving, and the engraving as it appeared in the *Illustrated London News*.

Although Simpson never attained his ambition of becoming a popular oil painter and respected Royal Academician, he took his job as artist-correspondent seriously. In the fiftieth anniversary number of the *Illustrated London News*, he expressed his feelings about his role eloquently: "As a Special Artist, I have at all times felt that I was not seeing for myself alone, but the others would see through my eyes, and that eyes yet unborn would, in the pages of the *Illustrated London News*, do the same."[2] EW

198

199

200 Robert Smith (1787-1873)

Inside the Main Entrance of the Purana Qila, Delhi, 1823?

Oil on canvas
30 ⁄16 x 42 in (81.9 x 107.3 cm)

B 1976.7.73

1 Burton Stein, *A History of India* (Oxford: Blackwell, 1998), pp.165-166.

A talented painter, Colonel Robert Smith made his way in India as a military engineer, architect and archaeologist. After a brief stint in Penang due to ill health, Smith returned to India as Garrison Engineer at Delhi, a post which invested him with the responsibility of preserving and, at times, restoring many of the monuments of this ancient city, such as the Jami Masjid and the Qutb Minar. These tasks induced him to paint a number of local architectural landmarks, of which the Purana Qila ("Old Fort") was one.

The fort was built by the renowned military and administrative genius Sher Shah. A member of the Suras, an Afghan clan which beset the Mughals frequently in the sixteenth century, Sher Shah ruled northern India briefly, from 1538 to 1545, when he died in battle. In 1545, the Sura empire extended from the five rivers of the Punjab to the eastern borders of the Ganges Delta.[1] Smith's view of the interior side of the fort's northern gate displays his close knowledge of the edifice, which had suffered severe damage over its first two and a half centuries. During his tenure as Garrison Engineer, Smith lived on the walls of the fort with an Indian mistress, a relationship that would have been considered scandalous by the small Anglo community in Delhi in the early nineteenth century. SV

201 Joseph Mallord William Turner (1775-1851)

Rome from Monte Mario, c. 1818

Watercolor
5 ½ x 8 ½ in. (14 x 21.6 cm)

B 1975.4.1424

1 An extensive Turner bibliography can be found in Martin Butlin and Evelyn Joll, *The Paintings of J.M.W. Turner*, revised edition (New Haven: Yale University Press, 1984). A more recent publication of particular pertinence in this context is Cecilia Powell, *Turner in the South: Rome, Naples, Florence* (New Haven: Yale University Press, 1987).

Although he did not venture as far afield as Roberts or Lear or a number of other painters and draftsmen, J.M.W. Turner was undoubtedly the greatest artist traveler of the nineteenth century. Trained in the eighteenth-century topographical tradition, he early transcended the limitations of that tradition. Yet the topographical element remained an important part of his art. John Ruskin would designate the most elevated and imaginative recording of reality as "Turnerian topography."

This watercolor of Rome, which was owned by Ruskin, is not the product of Turner's travels. It is one of eighteen watercolors that Turner worked up from drawings that the architect James Hakewill had made in Italy. This was before Turner had made his first visit to Italy in 1819, a visit much influenced by Hakewill's suggested itinerary. *Hakewill's Picturesque Tour in Italy*, published in 1820 with engravings after Turner's watercolors, would become a popular volume with tourists. In 1820 Turner painted his own view of the city from Monte Mario for his friend and patron Walter Fawkes (private collection).[1]

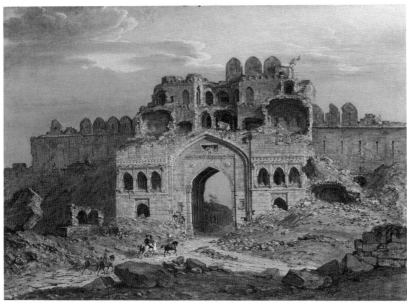

200

201

202 Joseph Mallord William Turner (1775-1851)

Venice, The Mouth of the Grand Canal,
c. 1840

Watercolor

8 ⅝ x 12 ½ in. (21.9 x 31.8 cm)

B 1977.14.4652

1   The question of a Venetian visit in the 1830s is thoroughly explored in Lindsay Stainton, *Turner's Venice* (London: British Museum Publications, 1985).

While Venetian subjects loom large in Turner's work, he visited the city no more than three times. During his first tour of Italy in 1819, he stayed briefly in Venice in September. Although he sketched there in pencil and watercolors, no oil paintings or finished watercolors immediately resulted from this visit. He seems to have returned to Venice in 1833, although there is no firm evidence. Beginning in that year, however, he did regularly contribute paintings of Venetian subjects to the exhibitions of the Royal Academy and continued to do so through 1846. He was definitely back in Venice from August 20 to September 3, 1840. In this two week span, he produced approximately sixty watercolors. None of these is elaborately finished, nor would Turner use them as the basis for producing finished watercolors, as he would with his Swiss watercolor sketches of the next few years. While most remained in Turner's possession and became part of his bequest to the nation, a number were acquired by his patrons. They are wonderfully evocative, light-filled, and ethereal.

203 Elijah Walton (1832-1880)

Portrait of the Artist's Dromedary, 1862

Watercolor over graphite

10 x 14 in. (25.4 x 35.6 cm)

Inscribed lower left: *Portrait of my dromedary / going to Sinai. 1862*; signed lower right: *Elijah Walton*

B 1977.14.4290

Although he also painted and published views of Norway, Wales, and the English Lakes, Walton was known primarily as a painter of Alpine and Middle Eastern scenery. Until 1860 he concentrated on genre subjects, but in that year, after marrying, he made his first trip to Egypt with his bride. She died of dysentery at the Second Cataract. Walton stayed on in the Middle East until August of 1862, traveling to Syria and Constantinople. Like Lear, Walton was fascinated by camels, actually publishing in 1865 a volume titled *The Camel: Its Anatomy, Proportions, and Paces.*

202

203

204 Elijah Walton (1832-1880)

Sasso di Pelmo as seen from St. Luzia, Tyrol, 1866

Watercolor and gouache over graphite
13 ¹³⁄₁₆ x 9 ⅞ in. (35.1 x 25.1 cm)

Inscribed verso: *Sasso di Pelmo / as seen from near St. Luzia Tyrol / May 1866. / Elijah Walton*

B 1975.4.1785

1 "In Memoriam. Elijah Walton, F.G.S.," *Alpine Journal*, vol. 10 (1880), p. 76.

From 1862 until his death, Walton was a frequent visitor to the Alps, which provided him with the subject matter for many of the watercolors he so prolifically produced. A number of these were reproduced by chromolithography as illustrations to a succession of books on Alpine topics. In an obituary in the *Alpine Journal*, T.G. Bonney, a geologist and fellow member of the Alpine Club, wrote: "It may be confidently asserted that no artist has ever painted a snow-peak with its slopes and cliffs and cornices with so much knowledge, so much power, and so much poetic feeling, as Elijah Walton." Bonney acknowledged that "Walton's colouring was peculiar," but maintained that "his perception of colour was exceptionally acute."[1]

205 Hugh William Williams (1773-1829)

View of the Forum in Rome, 1828

Watercolor over graphite with stopping-out, scraping out and gum
15 ⅞ x 25 ½ in. (40.3 x 64.8 cm)

Signed and dated lower right:
H. W. Williams / 1828

Paul Mellon Fund
B1978.16.2

1 See the account of Williams in David Irwin and Francina Irwin, *Scottish Painters at Home and Abroad, 1700-1900* (London: Faber and Faber, 1973), pp. 228-31.

2 Hugh William Williams, *Travels in Italy, Greece, and the Ionian Isles* (Edinburgh: Archibald Constable and Co., 1820), vol. 2, p. 302.

Born in Wales but educated and trained as an artist in Scotland, Williams made a tour of the Mediterranean in 1816 and 1817.[1] On his return he produced a detailed account of the trip, published in 1820 as *Travels in Italy, Greece, and the Ionian Isles*. In Edinburgh in 1822 he exhibited a group of watercolors worked up from his Greek sketches. The exhibition was a great success, and the strongly Turner-influenced watercolors were engraved and published in 1829 under the title *Select Views in Greece*. The artist has been known ever since as "Grecian" Williams. For much of his work of the 1820s, Williams continued to draw on his experiences of the classical landscapes of Greece and Italy, as in this late watercolor of the Roman Forum. Williams's fulsome account of his visit to the Forum suggests the response which such images were intended to elicit from contemporary viewers: "The triumphal arches, the remains of palaces and temples, addressing the mind thorugh every stain and every dye of crumbling and dejected ruin, their last shadows recalling to our contemplation Roman glory, Roman honour, Roman virtue, Roman genius, Roman cruelty and folly, formed a spectacle that spoke to the heart, and bade the eye obey its sad emotion."[2]

204

205

Selected Bibliography

The literature on Edward Lear is extensive; the following selection concentrates on his work as a topographical artist. Ann Colley's *Edward Lear and the Critics* provides a useful overview of all aspects of the Lear literature. The selection of books on aspects of travel and travel art focuses on publications of the last twenty years. Books and articles on individual artists may be found in the notes to the catalogue entries. Excluded here are the illustrated travel books of the eighteenth and nineteenth centuries. These are listed in *Travel in Aquatint and Lithography, 1770-1860, from the Library of J. R. Abbey.*

EDWARD LEAR

Colley, Ann C. *Edward Lear and the Critics.* Columbia, SC: Camden House, 1993.

Davidson, Angus. *Edward Lear, Landscape Painter and Nonsense Poet.* New York: Dutton, 1939.

Dehejia, Vidya. *Impossible Picturesqueness: Edward Lear's Indian Watercolours, 1873-1875,* exhibition catalogue. Ahmedabad: Mapin Publishing, 1988.

Fowler, Rowena, ed. *Edward Lear: The Cretan Journal.* Athens and Dedham: Denise Harvey and Co., 1984.

Hofer, Philip. *Edward Lear as a Landscape Draughtsman.* Cambridge, Massachusetts: Belknap Press of Harvard University Press, 1967.

Hyman, Susan, ed. *Edward Lear in the Levant: Travels in Albania, Greece, and Turkey in Europe 1848-1849.* London: John Murray, 1988.

Lear, Edward. *Letters of Edward Lear,* edited by Lady Constance Strachey. London: T. Fisher Unwin, 1907.

Lear, Edward. *Later Letters of Edward Lear,* edited by Lady Constance Strachey. London: T. Fisher Unwin, 1911.

Lear, Edward. *Selected Letters,* edited by Vivien Noakes. Oxford: Clarendon Press, 1988.

Murphy, Ray, ed. *Edward Lear's Indian Journal: Watercolours and Extracts from the Diary of Edward Lear 1873-1875.* London: Jarrolds, 1953.

Noakes, Vivien. *Edward Lear: The Life of a Wanderer.* London: Collins, 1968.

Noakes, Vivien. *Edward Lear, 1812-1888,* exhibition catalogue. London: Royal Academy, 1985.

Noakes, Vivien. *The Painter Edward Lear.* London: David and Charles, 1991.

Pitman, Ruth. *Edward Lear's Tennyson.* Manchester: Carcanet Press, 1988.

Sherrard, Philip, ed. *Edward Lear: The Corfu Years: A Chronicle Presented through His Letters and Journals.* Athens and Dedham: Denise Harvey and Co., 1988.

Tsigakou, Fani-Maria. *Edward Lear's Greece, from the Gennadeion Collections,* exhibition catalogue. Thessaloniki: Cultural Centre of Thessaloniki, 1997.

Archer, Mildred, and Lightbown, Ronald. *India Observed: India as Viewed by British Artists, 1760-1860*, exhibition catalogue. London: Victoria and Albert Museum, 1982.

Ackerman, Gerald M. *Les orientalistes de l'école britannique*. Courbevoie, Paris: ACR Édition Internationale, 1991.

Black, Jeremy. *The British Abroad: The Grand Tour in the Eighteenth Century*. New York: St. Martin's Press, 1992.

Brendon, Piers. *Thomas Cook: 150 Years of Popular Tourism*. London: Secker and Warburg, 1991.

Bull, Duncan. *Classic Ground: British Artists and the Landscape of Italy, 1740-1830*, exhibition catalogue. New Haven: Yale Center for British Art, 1981.

Buzard, James. *The Beaten Track: European Tourism, Literature and the Ways to Culture, 1800-1918*. Oxford and New York: Oxford University Press, 1993.

Chard, Chloe and Langdon, Helen, ed. *Transports: Travel, Pleasure and Imaginative Geography, 1600-1830*. Studies in British Art, vol. 3. New Haven and London: Yale University Press, 1996.

Clayton, Peter A. *The Rediscovery of Ancient Egypt: Artists and Travelers in the 19th Century*. London: Thames and Hudson, 1982.

Ingamells, John. *A Dictionary of British and Irish Travellers in Italy, 1701-1800*. New Haven and London: Yale University Press, 1997.

Llewellyn, Briony. *The Orient Observed: Images of the Middle East from the Searight Collection*. London: Victoria & Albert Museum, 1989.

Pal, Pratapaditya, and Dehejia, Vidya. *From Merchants to Emperors: British Artists and India, 1757-1930*. Ithaca and London: Cornell University Press, 1986.

Pemble, John. *The Mediterranean Passion: Victorians and Edwardians in the South*. Oxford: Clarendon Press, 1987.

Powell, Cecilia. *Italy in the Age of Turner: "The Garden of the World."* London: Merrell Holberton, 1998.

Stoneman, Richard. *A Luminous Land: Artists Discover Greece*. Los Angeles: The J. Paul Getty Museum, 1998.

Thornton, Lynne. *The Orientalists: Painter-travellers, 1828-1908*. Paris: ACR Edition, 1983.

Travel in Aquatint and Lithography, 1770-1860, from the Library of J. R. Abbey, 2 vols. London: Curwen Press, 1957.

Tsigakou, Fani-Maria. *The Rediscovery of Greece: Travellers and Painters of the Romantic Era*. London: Thames and Hudson, 1981.

Urry, John. *The Tourist Gaze: Leisure and Travel in Contemporary Societies*. London and Newbury Park: Sage Publications, 1990.

Visions of the Ottoman Empire, exhibition catalogue. Edinburgh: Scottish National Portrait Gallery, 1994.

Wilton, Andrew, and Bignamini, Ilaria, eds. *Grand Tour: The Lure of Italy in the Eighteenth Century*, exhibition catalogue. London: Tate Gallery, 1996.